In her fabulous way, Lily Ling brings fable, fairy-tale, and magical realism into International Relations, and makes of the discipline a set of alternat   he has become a n   **7000584554**   nd scholarship.

                                                                                          ind
                                                                                            JK

The wonderful thing about this book is that it is not concerned in speaking back to the West. Rather, its stories facilitate an apprehension of thought systems and sensibilities that are otherwise to the provincial vocabulary and imagination of International Relations. Don't just read it, inhabit it.

Robbie Shilliam, *Queen Mary,*
University of London, UK

At once fairy-tale and feminist/postcolonial critique, this highly unusual book rewards the open-minded reader with a creative new vision for world politics.

Roland Bleiker, *Professor of International Relations,*
University of Queensland, Australia

Ling's book is both a provocation and a mindful meditation on the play of wealth, power, love, security, and knowledge in politics; it disorients in a good way, suggesting new possibilities for understanding and changing world politics.

Neta C. Crawford, *Professor of Political*
Science, Boston University, USA

IMAGINING WORLD POLITICS

This book offers a non-Western feminist perspective on world politics and international relations. Creative, innovative, and challenging, it seeks completely to transform contemporary Eurocentric and masculinist IR by re-presenting it in non-Western, non-masculinist, and non-academic terms. Drawing on Daoist dialectics, the stories of Sihar and Shenya aim to redress such hegemonic imbalance by completing the IR story. To the *yang* of power politics, this book offers a *yin* of fairy-tale. (Both are equally fantastical but to different purposes.) To the *yang* of binary categories like Self vs Other, West vs Rest, hypermasculinity vs hyper-femininity, Sihar and Shenya show their *yin* complementarities and complicities, inside and out, top and bottom, center and periphery. And to the *yang* of intransigent hegemony, *Sihar & Shenya* explores the *yin* of emancipation through porous, water-like thought and behavior through venues like aesthetics and emotions. From this basis, we begin to see another world with another kind of politics.

Written with students of IR and world politics in mind, this book offers a postcolonial bridge for IR/WP. Following an academic introduction to assist the reader, Ling moves away from traditional scholarship and into three interlocking fables:

- Book I shows what an alternative world could look and feel like.
- Book II makes the implications for IR/WP more explicit. It draws on the traditional Chinese notion of the five movements (*wu xing*) – fire, metal, earth, wood, and water – to illustrate iconic elements of IR/WP – power, wealth, security, love, and knowledge – and how they could change according to circumstance and context.
- Epilogue/Introduction: The Return brings the reader back into the Western world and focuses on modern-day PhD student Wanda who is troubled by what she is learning, and searches for a different perspective.

Engaging with the substantive problematiques at the heart of international relations studies, this work is a unique and innovative resource for all students and scholars of international relations and world politics.

L.H.M. Ling is Associate Dean for Faculty Affairs at the New School for Public Engagement (NSPE) and Associate Professor of International Affairs, The New School. She is also author of *The Dao of World Politics: Towards a Post-Westphalian, Worldist International Relations* (Routledge, 2014).

Interventions

Edited by:

Jenny Edkins, Aberystwyth University and
Nick Vaughan-Williams, University of Warwick

'As Michel Foucault has famously stated, "knowledge is not made for understanding; it is made for cutting." In this spirit, the Edkins–Vaughan-Williams Interventions series solicits cutting-edge, critical works that challenge mainstream understandings in international relations. It is the best place to contribute post-disciplinary works that think rather than merely recognize and affirm the world recycled in IR's traditional geopolitical imaginary.'

Michael J. Shapiro, *University of Hawai'i at Mānoa, USA*

The series aims to advance understanding of the key areas in which scholars working within broad critical post-structural and postcolonial traditions have chosen to make their interventions, and to present innovative analyses of important topics.

Titles in the series engage with critical thinkers in philosophy, sociology, politics and other disciplines and provide situated historical, empirical and textual studies in international politics.

IMAGINING WORLD POLITICS

Sihar & Shenya, a fable for our times

L.H.M. Ling
The New School

Routledge
Taylor & Francis Group

LONDON AND NEW YORK

First published 2014
by Routledge
2 Park Square, Milton Park, Abingdon, Oxon OX14 4RN

and by Routledge
711 Third Avenue, New York, NY 10017

Routledge is an imprint of the Taylor & Francis Group, an informa business

British Library Cataloguing in Publication Data
A catalogue record for this book is available from the British Library

Library of Congress Cataloging in Publication Data
Ling, L. H. M.
  Imagining world politics: Sihar & Shenya, a fable for our times/
  L.H.M. Ling.
  pages cm – (Interventions)
  1. International relations. 2. World politics. 3. East and West.
  4. Feminism – Political aspects. 5. Feminist criticism. I. Title.
  JZ1242.L564 2014
  327 – dc23
  2013030518

ISBN: 978-0-415-71884-4 (hbk)
ISBN: 978-0-415-71886-8 (pbk)
ISBN: 978-1-315-86699-4 (ebk)

Typeset in Bembo, Stone Sans, Times New Roman, Courier New,
  Arial, Papyrus and Monaco
by Florence Production Limited, Stoodleigh, Devon, UK

This book is dedicated
to all the brothers and sisters in my life,
young and old, here and far away.

CONTENTS

The Fable of Sihar & Shenya

PREFACE

I conceived of *Sihar & Shenya* in New Delhi in 2009. While browsing through a bookstore, I came upon India's classic comic books, *amar chithra katha* (eternal picture stories). Generations of Indians have grown up with these books. With beautifully illustrated drawings, these tell of episodes from classic epics like the *Mahabharata* and *Ramayana* featuring India's pantheon of gods and goddesses along with contemporary political leaders like Dr. Ambedkar, the Dalit who rose to write India's Constitution. What a treasure trove I had discovered! I could not stop delighting in them, late into night, as I read each of the twenty or so *amar chithra katha* I had bought that day.

Within a few weeks, *Sihar & Shenya* started to take shape or, more accurately, took hold of me! The *amar chithra katha* resonated with classic Chinese epics like *Dream of the Red Chamber* (*honglou meng*), *The Romance of the Three Kingdoms* (*sanguo yanyi*), and *Journey to the West* (*xiyou ji*), as well as countless tales of emperors and empresses, generals and concubines, monks and abbesses. This combination of India and China proved heady, inviting, and utterly undeniable. I had to write *Sihar & Shenya*.

More than an exercise in creative writing, *Sihar & Shenya* gives students another world. It is not filtered through what we call "the West," "modernity," "realism," or "science." At the same time, the fable shows connections between the familiar and the alien, the past and the present, the East and the West.

What's behind *Sihar & Shenya*?

Sihar & Shenya is, essentially, a Daoist tale. As such, it reflects the Daoist principle of pairs.[1] Known as *yin* and *yang*, pairing in Daoism entails not just their differences but also their entwinements (see Figure P.1). That is, (big) differences push *yin* (the black sphere) and *yang* (the white sphere) apart. But (small) entwinements pull them together. *Yin* exists in *yang* (black-within-white) just as *yang* exists in *yin* (white-within-black). Hence, *yin* and *yang* cannot do without each other even as each opposes the other. Together, they constitute a whole – the circle in Figure P.1 – that is forever interacting and mutually transforming.

FIGURE P.1 Daoist dialectics: balanced *ying/yang* relations

In substantive terms, *yin* represents the female principle and *yang*, the male. Their pairing involves all those characteristics associated with femaleness and maleness: e.g., darkness/light, cold/hot, soft/hard, negative/positive. A critical reader might ask: who wants to be dark, cold, soft, and negative when one could be in the light, hot, hard, and positive? Herein lies the wisdom of the *dao*: femaleness and maleness co-create the world. The *Daodejing* (*Classic of the* Dao) cites the *dao* as the "sire of the many" (*zhongfu*) and the "mother of everything" (*wanwu zhi mu*).[2] "It should be noted," write Roger Ames and David Hall, "that mother is the impregnated female, and father is the siring male. Each of them entails the other."[3]

The Daoist whole thus *arises* from its parts. Accordingly, nothing stays the same. The whole constantly changes and transforms as its parts interact with each other due to dynamics both internal (*yin*-within-*yang*, *yang*-within-*yin*) and external (*yin* to *yang*, *yang* to *yin*). Yet these dynamics do not unfold indiscriminately or mechanistically, producing the same outcomes each time. That is, they are not reproducible or generalizable. *Yin/yang* dialectics lead to certain outcomes only under certain conditions.

The fable's two lead characters – Sihar and Shenya – exemplify this principle of *yin/yang* pairing. Each seems the other's opposite: one is male, sovereign of a kingdom, a ruler; the other is female, a priestess who specializes in trees, an advisor. Indeed, an ancient law prohibits any private relations between sovereign and priestess. Yet Sihar and Shenya match internally because each bears elements of the other within despite their external differences. One need only make a suggestion and the other would easily understand and carry it out. Such internal compatibility escapes the tyrant Norom, for instance. Even after kidnapping Shenya, hoping to learn of Sihar's success as a sovereign, Norom could not benefit from her counsels. "*Enough of this tree talk!*" he screams her short.

For Daoists, water exemplifies the *dao*.[4] "The highest efficacy," Laozi[5] states in the *Daodejing*, "is like water":

> It is because water benefits everything [*wanwu*]
> Yet views to dwell in places loathed by the crowd[6]
> That it comes nearest to proper way-making.[7]

And again:

> The meekest in the world
> Penetrates the strongest in the world . . .[8]

In other words, water shapes but does not coerce. And like water, Daoists teach, one must not intervene where natural, organic processes are in play. To do so would not only distort and lead to excess of one kind or another, but it would also presume too much. No one has a god's-eye view.

Indeed, Daoist dialectics begin with a fundamental respect or ontological parity for the world's "myriad things" (*wanwu*). Only on this basis could the world experience justice and compassion for all. Shenya shows Sihar, for example, how he can learn from Nature to rule his kingdom. When Norom threatens war, Shenya draws on the principle of trees to help Sihar devise a plan to defeat Norom without shedding one drop of blood. Similarly, Sihar enhances in Shenya a part of herself previously not considered. She thinks her calling at the Temple of Knowledge as noble as that of wife and mother – until she meets Sihar. A love naturally blooms between them but they could not enjoy it simply as a private, personal happiness. To remain true, the love must respect the context that gives rise to it in the first place – and this involves, as underscored in Book II, several lives as well as lifetimes, not just the two lovers in the moment.

Whether one believes in reincarnation or not, the point is that we do not sprout, as Hobbes described, like mushrooms after a rain.[9] Human life simply does not and cannot map onto asocial fungi. Instead, we are endowed with what the late Paul Feyerabend called a "richness of being."[10] It defies neat categorizations as proposed by some social scientists. Let us acknowledge our legacies and their special nature: that is, they are personal *and* social, individual *and* collective, ancient *and* contemporary. At the same time, change runs through these legacies as a constant. They do not stand still, nor do we. Our fates, like those of Sihar and Shenya, twist and turn but always within a context of meaning infused by our received legacies.

To make sense of such constancy-within-change and change-within-constancy, we need aesthetics.[11] Artistic expression helps us to inhabit change while appreciating its disruptive stimulations. In the *Zhuangzi*,[12] for example, creativity best realizes the *dao*. "To be fully integrative," observes Roger Ames on the *Zhuangzi*, "individuals must overcome the sense of discreteness and discontinuity with their environment, and they must contribute personally and creatively to the emerging pattern and regularity of existence called *dao*."[13] That is, aesthetics bridge action with ethics with a state of being. Simply knowing and doing right are not enough, one must also *feel* it: "[A]ny 'ethical' judgments in the narrow sense are going to be derived from aesthetic sensibilities – the intensity, integrity, and appropriateness that one detail has for its environing elements as interpreted from some particular perspective."[14]

A famous anecdote from the *Zhuangzi* illustrates this point.[15] It tells of a conversation between Master Zhuang and his dear friend and intellectual sidekick Hui Shi. Strolling on a bridge over the River Hao one fine day, Master Zhuang remarks that the fishes must be enjoying themselves. "How do *you* know," challenges Hui Shi, "since you're not a fish?" In effect, Master Zhuang replies: "How do you know I don't know? And the fact that you asked me how I know must mean that you suspect I know. I know because I'm standing here over this bridge relishing the day, the conversation, and the fishes." In other words, explains Roger Ames, "[i]t is the situation rather than some discrete agent that is properly described (and prescribed) as happy."[16] Master Zhuang takes in the general wonderfulness of the day so he extrapolates that the fishes, too, must be happy. Otherwise, how could everything feel so right?

Similarly, I wrote *Sihar & Shenya* because it simply felt so right.

Why do we need *Sihar & Shenya* in IR/WP?

All this is fine and good, one could say, but why do we need Daoist dialectics in International Relations (IR)/World Politics (WP) and, especially, in the form of a fable like *Sihar & Shenya*?

My answer, in brief, is this: IR/WP, as currently conceived and practiced, suffers from a debilitating imbalance. Daoist dialectics can help us understand how and why, as well as what we can do about it.

IR/WP, in short, is all *yang* and no *yin*. In their survey of the top 23 IR departments in the US and Europe, Jonas Hagmann and Thomas Biersteker find a predominant pattern in IR syllabi in terms of methodology (rationalist/formal), language (English), geographical location of authors (US), and their gender (male).[17] Some European institutions, like those in France and Italy, may include histories and perspectives from their localities but *no* teaching exists of non-Western, non-masculinist approaches to the world, world politics, or IR.

Yet the *yins* of the world make IR/WP.[18] These come through intellectual appropriations, such as the use of native informants to explain a particular part of the world whenever it fails to comply with the status quo, as well as structural exploitations, such as the transatlantic slave trade that enriched and militarized white rule.[19] Both serve liberal-capitalism as world order even when the price of admission for most requires an historical erasure. This collective amnesia works doubly: the subaltern must forget not only the violence that made "modernity" possible in the first place but also the ingenuity of local hybridities in response to it.[20]

Here, IR/WP manifests a second imbalance: the pursuit of "science" at the expense of the "social" for a field rife with humanity.[21] Even before behavioralism and its rationalist/formal methodology reigned supreme, IR/WP as defined by the inter-state, Westphalian tradition reduced all politics to discrete calculi of state power. Indeed, IR/WP glorifies such instrumental logic as the exemplar of human rationality even while perpetrating irrational, inhumane violence onto colonized Others, whether "at home" or "over there."[22] In effect, Westphalian IR/WP declares to the Other: "We lead, you follow. Otherwise, you will never catch up with us economically, militarily, politically, and culturally. (And, by the way, we have no intention of ever letting you catch up – and you know it. Isn't hegemony grand?)"[23] Such is the epistemic violence that comes with Westphalian world politics.[24]

Lost is any sense of politics or humanity beyond state power. We forget the value of a day spent with a friend engaged in lively conversation about the feelings of fishes. In all the scurrying for power, we fail to ask: what is it *for*, to benefit *whom*, and at *whose* cost? Most crucially, we begin to turn away from ourselves. We avoid asking: do we agree with this vision for ourselves and for generations to come?[25]

A third imbalance, already suggested, underpins the first two. Westphalian IR/WP dichotomizes the masculine from the feminine, then skews the relationship such that the former (identified with the West, science, reason, power) always supersedes the latter (identified with the Rest, religion, emotion, weakness). This asymmetry deprives the feminine from ever achieving parity with the masculine; more egregiously, it permits the masculine to abuse the feminine despite the former's *intimate* dependence on the latter for labor, resources, ideas, poetry, memory, and other reminders of humanity.[26]

Given these imbalances, Westphalian IR/WP cannot offer any kind of justice. Neither philosophically nor institutionally does the field recognize its relations with or contributions from Others, despite ample evidence to the contrary.[27] Some IR scholars may acknowledge the increasingly "global" nature of contemporary problems in world politics but they still tote the same concepts, theories, methods, and practices. Stephen Gill calls it an "imperial common sense."[28] It insists that we live in one world only and it is necessarily white, male, and Westphalian. Hypermasculine whiteness thus locks us in with no way out.[29] Realists accept it as the "tragedy" of great power politics.[30]

Many in IR/WP disagree. Critical theorists like constructivists, postcolonialists, and feminists deconstruct such Self-aggrandizing vanities.[31] They demand an accounting for the subalternized, feminized Other who had little to do with creating these "tragedies" yet must pick up the pieces after the havoc wreaked by the privileged, hypermasculine egos of Westphalian IR/WP.[32]

Sihar & Shenya offers an alternative. It aims to redress the hegemonic imbalance in IR/WP by offering a complementary story. To the *yang* of realist power politics, *Sihar & Shenya* presents a *yin* of fairy-tale. (Both are equally fantastical but to different purposes.) To the *yang* of binary categories like Self vs Other, West vs Rest, hypermasculinity vs hyperfemininity, *Sihar & Shenya* shows their *yin* complicities, inside and out, top and bottom, center and periphery. Notions of time in the fable, for example, do not stay in their categorical boxes of "past," "present," and "future," but interweave with the presence of each in the other, suggesting to the reader that we have an agency to interpret and re-interpret received legacies. To the *yang* of intransigent hegemony, *Sihar & Shenya* explores the *yin* of emancipation through porous, water-like transformations. And we begin to see another world with another kind of politics. Compassion and care motivated by respect, this fable suggests, can bring about justice that sustains over time.

But first and foremost, we must account for past trespasses against both the Other *and* the Self. Simply avenging past violence with more violence or redressing inequities through legislation only cannot "settle" old scores. Rather, as *Sihar & Shenya* suggests, justice involves a never-ending process of negotiation, sometimes even with the gods.

One could ask why *this* fable for *this* exercise? Epics abound for us to study, and these have been around for centuries, if not millennia. Indeed, many analyze these ancient texts as well as modern classics like *The Lord of the Rings* for insight into IR/WP.[33] What does *Sihar & Shenya* offer that these do not? I wrote this fable specifically with the IR/WP student in mind. In this sense, the fable presents what never existed before: a postcolonial bridge for IR/WP.

A postcolonial bridge

Currently, corporate giants like Disney/Pixar and DreamWorks dominate the public's fantastical images about the Other. They produce clever animated features like *Teenage Mutant Ninja Turtles* (1990, 2014), *Aladdin* (1992), *Mulan* (1998, 2004), and *Kung Fu Panda* (2008, 2011, 2016) that tell about the non-Western (and, in two cases, non-human) Other in ways identifiable to the US/Western public. As such, these animated features may seek to close the gap between Self and Other; but they also deprive the viewer of knowing about the Other *on its own terms*. Instead, the Other is presented in the guise of familiar American motifs, actions, and personas. And if, in real life, the Other is shockingly not so, alienation sets in. This begins at an early age, since viewers tend to be children who grow up with these images as part of their cultural consciousness.

The alienation cuts both ways. Many of these animated features, like *Kung Fu Panda* for example, are translated into Other languages like Chinese. Hollywood's rendition of the world socializes young viewers from outside the West to view the West, accordingly, through similar stereotypes and caricatures. Of course, there are alternatives like Japan's exemplary *animé*, *Spirited Away* (2001). But such films are so fanciful that the viewer cannot easily draw implications for IR/WP.

Put differently, *Sihar & Shenya* expresses in fictional form the real-life linkages that have always bound us even as they distinguish us. These involve journeys through time (past–present–future), space (human world, world of gods and spirits, East and West), self (individual, community, cosmos), and knowledge (secular/profane, particular/universal, ordinary/extraordinary), and how each cumulates and "returns" in cyclical yet open ways, with negative or positive effects, depending on how one chooses to deal with life's challenges. To underscore this point, I match the traditional Chinese notion of the five movements (*wu xing*) – fire, metal, earth, wood, and water – with five iconic elements in IR/WP – power, wealth, security, love, and knowledge. Both sets of elements change in impact and meaning over time, across circumstance and through their interactions.

Sihar & Shenya shows what an alternative world could look and feel like. Book I introduces it; Book II connects it with IR/WP more directly. And the Epilogue/Introduction brings the reader full circle as it refers back to Book I but through the context of a contemporary character in the West named Wanda. As *Sihar & Shenya* underscores, time circles and interweaves past–present–future. So, too, could the reader of this volume. The general reader could begin at the beginning to savor Book I's alternative world. But the student of IR/WP, more used to academic texts and their linear mode of reasoning, could begin at the end. The Epilogue/Introduction concludes this volume but it also begins it. Similarly, Book II could be read in any order to the others. Like *dim sum*, this volume has no set beginning, middle, or end. It offers a ceaseless flow of carts carrying treats and ends only when the diners decide to leave.

Sihar & Shenya also aims to reach, paradoxically, those from outside the geographical West.[34] As John Hobson has shown, Eurocentrism still dominates theorizing in IR/WP even after three centuries of development.[35] Postcolonial and feminist scholars have written extensively on the nature of and consequences to this intellectual hegemony,[36] but they have yet to articulate an alternative paradigm to Hobbesian-based, Westphalian-framed IR.[37] Their critique remains a critique. Some attempt to "reverse the gaze" from East to West but these efforts tend to elude mass interest due to an overly academic – or, as some see it, religious – orientation.[38] Critical IR also tends to be relegated to the Humanities. Edward Said tried to bridge this gap by unveiling the politics in literature.[39] But few can instantiate what Roland Bleiker has urged as an "aesthetic turn" to IR/WP,[40] although many have responded to its thrilling call.[41] Consequently, theorists and policy-makers alike still hew to the hegemony of one approach to IR/WP, reproducing its violence through the usual ultimatum ("convert to be like us or suffer our discipline") or reactions against it ("Death to America!").[42]

In sum, this fable seeks to expand the reader's imagination about what is possible, not just what is practical. E.H. Carr was right that world affairs are too important to leave to a few, hide-bound "experts."[43] IR as a discipline needs to democratize. One way of doing so is to speak directly to the public and in a way that is generally accessible.

I hope you find this fable entertaining yet thought-provoking, a tale of transformation redolent with eternal verities, and a guide to justice as well as love.

Please note all references to Hobbes in the Epilogue/ Introduction come from *The Leviathan* and *De Cive*. I cite Pushmataha's speech here,[44] as with the Wôpanâak Language Reclamation Project,[45] so as not to disrupt the flow of storytelling in the Epilogue/Introduction. The same applies to references to the Coyote in native American culture.[46] Readers interested in learning more about the Andean cosmovision and the political movements it has inspired could consult Chapter Nine of *The* Dao *of World Politics*.

Enjoy and be well.

L.H.M. Ling
New York
2013

Notes

1   For a more academic treatment of Daoism in and for International Relations (IR), see L.H.M. Ling, *The* Dao *of World Politics: Towards a Post-Westphalian, Worldist International Relations*, London: Routledge, 2014.
2   Roger T. Ames and David L. Hall, *Daodejing, "Making this Life Significant": A Philosophical Translation*, New York: Ballantine Books, 2003, p. 109. I prefer this version given their philosophical interpretation of the *Daodejing*, not just its linguistic translation.
3   *Ibid*.
4   From ancient times, many have appreciated water's philosophical and practical properties. Note this observation:

>   Thales, the first Greek philosopher, declared water the first principle of all things. The Greek poet Pindar called water "the best of all things." An Indian *Purana* praises water as "the source of all things and existence." Sounding somewhat like a Daoist, St. Francis celebrated water as the mirror of nature and the model of his conduct.

>   Kirill Ole Thompson, "'What Is the Reason of Failure or Success? The Fisherman's Song Goes Deep into the River': Fishermen in the *Zhuangzi*," in Roger T. Ames (ed.), *Wandering at Ease in the*

Zhuangzi, Albany: State University of New York Press, 1998, p. 18.

5 Laozi is variously identified as someone who lived in the sixth century BCE or serves as a composite of historical figures from fifth–fourth centuries BCE.

6 In other words, water does not discriminate between the high and the low, the desired and the unwanted, the sacred and the profane.

7 Ames and Hall, *Daodejing, op. cit.*, p. 87.

8 For example, water can shape rock. The *Laozi* cited by Thompson, "What is the Reason of Failure or Success?" in Ames (ed.), *Wandering at Ease in the Zhuangzi, op. cit.*, p. 17.

9 "Let us return again to the state of nature, and consider men as if but even now sprung out of the earth, and suddainly (like Mushromes) come to full maturity without all kind of engagement to each other . . ." (Thomas Hobbes, Chapter VIII, *De Cive*). Online. Available <http://www.constitution.org/th/decive08.htm> (accessed 27 May 2013).

10 Paul Feyerabend, *Conquest of Abundance: A Tale of Abstraction versus the Richness of Being*, Chicago: University of Chicago Press, 1999.

11 Following Edward Said, Krishna finds the novel more telling of the nation than the state. Sankaran Krishna, "IR and the Postcolonial Novel: Nation and Subjectivity in India," in Sanjay Seth (ed.), *Postcolonial Theory and International Relations: A Critical Introduction*, London: Routledge, 2013, pp. 124–43.

12 Both the *Laozi* ("Master Lao"), supposed author of the *Daodejing*, and the *Zhuangzi* ("Master Zhuang") were compiled around the fourth–third centuries BCE but edited into their current form around the second century BCE. Laozi was perhaps a mystical persona who never existed. Master Zhuang or Zhuang Zhou was an iconoclast who lived in the fourth century BCE. Roger T. Ames, "Introduction," in Ames (ed.), *Wandering at Ease in the Zhuangzi, op. cit.*, p. 1.

13 *Ibid.*, p. 4.

14 *Ibid.*, p. 5.

15 Roger T. Ames, "Knowing in the *Zhuangzi*: 'From Here, Over the Bridge, on the River Hao'," *op. cit.*, pp. 219–30.

16 *Ibid.*, p. 221.

17 Jonas Hagmann and Thomas J. Biersteker, "Beyond the Published Discipline: Towards a Critical Pedagogy of International Studies," *European Journal of International Relations*, 2012, 1–40.

18 The very origin of sovereignty as a concept, Hobson argues, comes from interactions between the East and the West. John M. Hobson, "The Other Side of the Westphalian Frontier," in Seth (ed.), *Postcolonial Theory and International Relations*, *op. cit.*, pp. 32–48.

19 Anna M. Agathangelou and L.H.M. Ling, "The House of IR: From Family Politics to the *Poeisis* of Worldism," *International Studies Review*, 6, 4, December 2004, 21–49; John M. Hobson, *The Eastern Origins of Western Civilisation*, Cambridge: Cambridge University Press, 2004; Branwen Gruffydd Jones, "Slavery, Finance and International Political Economy: Postcolonial Reflections," in Seth (ed.), *Postcolonial Theory and International Relations*, *op. cit.*, pp. 49–69.

20 L.H.M. Ling, *Postcolonial International Relations: Conquest and Desire between Asia and the West*, London: Palgrave Macmillan, 2002; Sanjay Seth, "Postcolonial Theory and the Critique of International Relations," in Seth (ed.), *Postcolonial Theory and International Relations*, *op. cit.*, pp. 15–31.

21 See, for example, Ashis Nandy (ed.), *Science, Hegemony and Violence: A Requiem for Modernity*, 4th edition, Tokyo: United Nations University, 1996.

22 Ashis Nandy, *The Intimate Enemy: The Psychology of Colonialism*, Delhi: Oxford, 1988; Anthony Marx, *Making Race and Nation: A Comparison of the United States, South Africa, and Brazil*, Cambridge: Cambridge University Press, 1998; Geeta Chowdhry and Sheila Nair (eds), *Power, Postcolonialism, and International Relations: Reading Race, Gender, Class*, London: Routledge, 2002; Branwen Gruffydd Jones (ed.), *Decolonizing International Relations*, London: Rowman & Littlefield, 2006.

23 See, for example, Stephen Greenblatt, *Marvelous Possessions: The Wonder of the New World*, Chicago: University of Chicago Press, 1991. Greenblatt demonstrates that, even when the *conquistadores* thought they had absolutely nothing in common with the natives of the New World and enslaved them accordingly, the Spanish were projecting their own selves onto the natives thereby inverting the hegemonic gaze. In effect, Greenblatt writes, the natives highlighted to the *conquistadores* and their European Enlighten-ment brethren that "[w]e are all incomplete and unsteady, we are go-betweens, we do not know whom God loves and whom He hates" (*ibid.*, p. 150). See also, Christine Helliwell and Barry Hindess, "Time and the Others," in Seth (ed.), *Postcolonial Theory and International Relations*, *op. cit.*, pp. 70–84.

24 John M. Hobson, *The Eurocentric Conception of World Politics: Western International Relations Theory, 1760–2010*, Cambridge: Cambridge University Press, 2012; Siba N'Zatioula Grovogui, "Deferring Difference: A Postcolonial Critique of the 'Race Problem' in Moral Thought," in Seth (ed.), *Postcolonial Theory and International Relations, op. cit.*, pp. 106–23.

25 For one version of this meditation, see Mustapha Kamal Pasha, "The 'Bandung Impulse' and International Relations," in Seth (ed.), *Postcolonial Theory and International Relations, op. cit.*, pp. 144–65.

26 Not all state relations, argues Shilliam, proceed from instrumental logic. Some reflect an older, grander worldview of generosity and hospitality, especially during times of crisis. He refers to Guyana's donation to Haiti after the 2010 earthquake that amounted to 80 times the US contribution. Robbie Shilliam, "The Spirit of Exchange," in Seth (ed.), *Postcolonial Theory and International Relations, op. cit.*, pp. 166–82. See also Marianne Marchand and Anne Sisson Runyan (eds), *Gender and Global Restructuring: Sightings, Sites, and Resistances*, 2nd edition, London: Routledge, 2011.

27 Besides the works already cited in this Preface, see Martin Bernal, *Black Athena: The Afroasiatic Roots of Classical Civilization* (The Fabrication of Ancient Greece 1765–1985, Volume 1), New Jersey: Rutgers University Press, 1987; Paul Gilroy, *The Black Atlantic: Modernity and Double-Consciousness*, Cambridge: Harvard University Press, 1993; Arturo Escobar, *Encountering Development: The Making and Unmaking of the Third World*, Princeton: Princeton University Press, 1996; Pinar Bilgin, "The International Political 'Sociology of a not so International Discipline'," *International Political Sociology*, 3, 3, 2009, 338–42; Geeta Chowdhry and Shirin Rai, "Geographies of Exclusion and the Politics of Inclusion: Race-Based Exclusions in the Teaching of International Relations," *International Studies Perspectives*, 10, 1, 2009, 84–91.

28 Stephen Gill, "Towards a Radical Concept of Praxis: Imperial 'Common Sense' versus the Post-Modern Prince," *Millennium: Journal of International Studies*, 40, 3, 2012, 505–24.

29 "Hypermasculinity" refers to distortions or exaggerations of what are identified as masculine traits; "hyperfemininity," the same regarding feminine ones. Targeting "hypermasculinity" does not mean elimination of masculinity in favor of femininity; rather, it means recognizing an imbalance between the two. L.H.M. Ling,

"Hypermasculinity," *Routledge International Encyclopedia of Women's Studies*, London: Routledge, 2001, pp. 1089–91.

30 John Mearsheimer, *The Tragedy of Great Power Politics*, New York: W.W. Norton, 2001.

31 I do not include Marxists/neo-Marxists (Gramscians) or post-modernists despite their critical premises. These theorists tend to reproduce hegemonic ways of thinking either by not questioning the cultural origins and applications of their concepts (like hegemony) or by leaving *de facto* power intact in their claims of "off-shore" theorizing. See, for example, L.H.M. Ling, "Hegemony and the Internationalizing State: A Postcolonial Analysis of China's Integration into Asian Corporatism," *Review of International Political* Economy, 3, 1, Spring 1996, 1–26; Anna M. Agathangelou and L.H.M. Ling, "Postcolonial Dissidence within Dissident IR: Transforming Master Narratives of Sovereignty in Greco-Turkish Cyprus," *Studies in Political Economy*, 54, 1, September 1997, 7–38.

32 Tarak Barkawi, "War, Armed Forces and Society in Postcolonial Perspective," in Seth (ed.), *Postcolonial Theory and International Relations*, *op. cit.*, pp. 87–105.

33 Abigail E. Ruane and Patrick James, *The International Relations of Middle-earth: Learning from* The Lord of the Rings, Ann Arbor: University of Michigan Press, 2012.

34 For example, the Graduate Institute of Political Science at National Sun Yat-sen University in Kaohsiung, Taiwan has dismantled its collection of Sun Yat-sen thought, even though the university was named after him. University higher-ups decided that Sun Yat-sen thought was no longer "relevant" to a world dominated by Western liberal theory. Private communication with a former director of the Center for Sun Yat-sen Thought.

35 Hobson, *The Eurocentric Conception of World Politics*, *op. cit.*

36 For a critical review of this literature, see Geeta Chowdhry and L.H.M. Ling, "Race(ing) Feminist IR: A Critical Overview of Postcolonial Feminism," in Robert A. Denemark (ed.), *The International Studies Encyclopedia*, London: Blackwell Publishing, 2010, pp. 6038–57. See also Robbie Shilliam (ed.), *International Relations and Non-Western Thought: Imperialism, Colonialism and Investigations of Global Modernity*, London: Routledge, 2011.

37 For greater elaboration of this argument, see Ling, *The* Dao *of World Politics*, *op. cit.*

38   See, for example, Rajiv Malhotra, *Being Different: An Indian Challenge to Western Universalism*, New Delhi: HarperCollins, 2011.

39   Edward Said, *Culture and Imperialism*, New York: Alfred A. Knopf, 1993.

40   Roland Bleiker, *Aesthetics and World Politics*, London: Palgrave Macmillan, 2009.

41   See, for example, "Political Aesthetics of Power and Protest," a workshop held at the University of Warwick, 25 September 2012. One early exception is a special issue of *Alternatives*, 25, 3, 2000, edited by Roland Bleiker, in which IR scholars published their poetry. Another space of exception in IR is the "Conversations" section of the *International Feminist Journal of Politics* (*IFjP*) that occasionally publishes poetry along with paintings, interviews, and other kinds of essays.

42   L.H.M. Ling, "Can the West Listen?" *Kulturaustausch* (*Journal for International Perspectives*), 4, 12, 2012, 72–74; L.H.M. Ling, "Neoliberal Neocolonialism: Comparing Enron with Asia's 'Crony Capitalism'," in Dirk Wiemann, Agata Stopinska, Anke Bartels, and Johannes Angermüller (eds), *Discourses of Violence – Violence of Discourses: Critical Interventions, Transgressive Readings and Postnational Negotiations*, Frankfurt/Main: Peter Lang, 2005, pp. 93–105; and Anna M. Agathangelou and L.H.M. Ling, "Power and Play through *Poisies*: Reconstructing Self and Other in the 9/11 Commission Report," *Millennium: Journal of International Studies*, 33, 3, 2005, 827–53.

43   E.H. Carr, *Twenty Years' Crisis: 1919–1939: An Introduction to the Study of International Relations*, latest edition, Basingstoke: Palgrave Macmillan, 2001.

44   Pushmataha, "He Whose Passions Are Inflamed by Military Success, Elevated Too High By a Treacherous Confidence, Hears No Longer the Dictates of Judgement," in Jerry D. Blanche (ed.), *Native American Reader: Stories, Speeches, Poems*, Juneau: The Denali Press, 1990, pp. 79–83.

45   Jeffrey Mifflin, "Saving a Language," *Technology Review*, 22 April 2008. Online. Available <http://www.technologyreview.com/article/409990/saving-a-language/page/3/> (accessed 29 May 2013).

46   Dawn E. Bastian and Judy K. Mitchell, *Handbook of Native American Mythology*, Santa Barbara: ABC-CLIO, 2004, pp. 76–83.

FOREWORD

The Awakening

John M. Hobson

"What's this book all about?" Thomas asks his classmate testily. "Looks more like a novel than a serious contribution to IR or postcolonial theory."

"Haven't you done the reading yet?" Sushila replies, surprised. "You should do. I'm glad I did . . . Really enjoyed it. Book I moved me to tears . . . A deeply moving story."

Typical female response – vague and over-emotional, dismisses Thomas. Definitely not what he wants to hear. Hoping to hop over to the nearest pub, Thomas wonders if he could just go to the last section of the book. It claims to summarize the first two sections and discuss IR more directly.

"What did you make of the Epilogue/Introduction?" he probes.

"I thought it all very useful, especially when read in conjunction with some of the author's other works. A good place to start would be a recent journal article of hers," replies Sushila.[1]

Dear God, more reading! Ugh.

"Presumably," Thomas cuts in, "it's all about empire, the international politics of subordination and domination, and bringing Eastern voices back in . . . All that kind of poco stuff?"

"Kind of . . . but not exactly," Sushila replies vaguely, much to Thomas's growing frustration. "Actually," she explains, "I read the Epilogue/Introduction first. The author says in the Preface that one could read out of order. I'm glad I did. I was in from the first moment. It spoke to me – I felt the author had written the book just for me. It was so elevating. I mean, here I am, a brown, non-Western woman confronted with a whole load of IR, which seems to speak a foreign language, usually penned by Anglo-Saxon males – no offense. Like Wanda in this story, I too felt alienated when beginning my degree. I too nearly gave it all up. But unlike Wanda, I was lucky to have read one of Ling's books: *Postcolonial International Relations*, particularly the first chapter.[2] From there, I entered the world of postcolonial international thought."

"But I *am* white, Western, and male," Thomas interjects. "Does this mean none of this will speak to me?" *In which case, why on earth should I bother reading it all?*

"Therein lies the rub," replies Sushila. "This book is probably more relevant for someone like yourself."

Still way too vague. Drat 'n double drat!

At this moment, responding to what feels like Thomas's bullying, Sushila pipes up with the dreaded words:

"The usual literature won't help. This book opens up new ground." She adds: "To be honest, Thomas, you're better off reading it for yourself. It's a fab read. You won't be disappointed."

Yeah, right! Realizing he isn't going to get his own way, Thomas cuts his losses, thanks Sushila curtly, and sets off for home, swearing and muttering to himself all the way.

Back in his flat, Thomas sits down and opens up the book. He reads the first two pages. *Oh God*, he winces. He continues a bit, checking down at the page number. *Only page 5? Uggghhh!* But Thomas perseveres . . . page 20. *Hmmm, this is actually quite interesting.* By the mid-20s he's in. He's captivated. Page numbers no longer matter.

When he finishes Book I, it's 10pm and dark outside. In three short hours, his mind-set has undergone a complete transformation. His earlier reluctance has given way to elation one moment and tears the next as he reads through the gripping twists and turns of *Sihar & Shenya*. He is simply blown away by such a beautiful story – its depth and exquisite storytelling, not to mention the cliff-hanger at the end.

Truth be told, Thomas has not applied himself to this particular module. Sure, some of it has been interesting, though challenging intellectually and, most of all, identity-wise. After all, he is a white Westerner. On occasion, he feels, resentfully, that this seems more like a crime against global humanity than a badge of honor; a feeling that reinforces his unwillingness to engage with the readings and arguments of the module. Much has been too "right on" (politically correct) for his comfort. A bright kid, Thomas has relied on his innate intelligence more than doing the assigned reading.

But now something has changed. Suddenly the module has come to life. And for once, he wants to get involved in the discussion. Next morning, Thomas walks determinedly to the seminar . . . for the first time in his three-year university experience.

"What did you think of the reading this week?" asks the Professor.

"I now understand!" blurts out Thomas.

"Understand what, Thomas?"

"We . . . together . . . must *feel* our way to a better future."

"What do you mean?"

"What we think is self-interest actually imprisons us into building up armies against imaginary Others, leading them to do the same – *ad infinitum* and *ad nauseam* – rendering us all ever more insecure and unhappy, producing a futile, self-fulfilling prophecy."

"We are not, as realists suggest, billiard balls?"

"No, Professor. *Sihar & Shenya* recognizes that there is more – much more. By restoring the expunged Other, we can reclaim our whole selves. Neither our identities nor our interests are fixed and exclusive."

"What's this to do with IR theory?" challenges Stephen, another student.

"Everything," replies Thomas. "*Sihar & Shenya* thinks through *how* we can move beyond the sterility, insecurity, and unhappiness of Westphalian world politics towards a brighter future of peace and, above all, happiness and love. Only by recognizing that agency is not the monopolistic preserve of the West but is expressed through multiple channels that serve to inter-weave East and West into a shared community of fate can we break out of our self-imposed prison of Self *versus* Other." Thomas basks in the Professor's beaming smile.

After class, Thomas returns home and straight to Book II. He is not disappointed. Elation returns once more. He opens an old, dusty journal and writes the first entry of what would turn out to be many in the years to come:

3 May 2013

Love can awaken even the lazy, one-eyed monster of Eurocentric IR.

Notes

1   L.H.M. Ling, "Worlds Beyond Westphalia: Daoist Dialectics and the 'China Threat'," *Review of International Studies*, 39, 3, 2013, 549–68.
2   L.H.M. Ling, *Postcolonial International Relations: Conquest and Desire between Asia and the West*, Houndmills: Palgrave Macmillan, 2002.

The Fable of Sihar & Shenya

as told to L.H.M. Ling

BOOK I: THE ORCHID AND THE TREE

* * *

Hello, Gentle Friend! What brings you to these parts? Our fine air and mountains? Yes, they are magical, aren't they?

Some biscuits with your *chai*? Travel is elixir to the soul, I say, but gruel for the body.

Lay down your burdens, Gentle Friend, if only for the moment. Let me tell you a wonderful and wondrous story. It's a story full of . . . Well, you'll find out as we go along. (More *chai*?)

Our story takes place in a Kingdom from long ago and far away. Or, it could be from right here, dreamed only yesterday . . . No matter.

It begins with the death of a Queen . . .

* * *

Sihar, the King

King Sihar steps wearily from her bed. "The Queen has passed," he tells the room, filled with family, friends, ministers, courtiers, and handmaidens. All weep quietly.

That night, Sihar bears vigil by the large, open window in the royal chamber. It overlooks the palace gardens with the roses and magnolia trees. The night is cool with glittering stars but Sihar cannot eat, cannot rest, cannot speak even. His children and others regard him with concern but they know best to leave him be. And they do, retiring from the King's chamber, one by one, as he remains by the window like a marble monument to the gods. Princess Salimar is the last to leave, casting her father a long, worried look.

By dawn's misty light, Sihar collapses to bed at last. Through sheer exhaustion, he slips into a dream. A jumble of images flashes before him. He sees their wedding day – the musicians bleating on their reed pipes, the dancers pounding on their drums as they whirl and twirl, the people cheering and jostling, the Royal Guards tall and proud on their steeds. She is veiled behind a garland of jasmine buds; he, sashed in green-and-white silk, atop an immense elephant approaching her dais, lumberingly, steadily, while his heart beats wildly and desperately.

The dream shifts to the birth of their son, Jandar, four years later; Salimar, a year after that. Patches of a life lived together flit by – the good, the bad, and the simply everyday.

A cool, calm lake emerges. Its water shimmers in the moon's golden glow. A sense of peace descends upon the dream and its dreamer.

Suddenly, Duan, Sihar's old steed, appears! The stallion is in his prime, muscles and sinews twitching in the dewy morn, eager for a ride. Duan's ears are perked up, as if to ask: "What are you waiting for?" The scene widens and Sihar sees that Duan is pawing an unknown field in an unknown country. High mountains capped with white loom from behind. Floppy flowers of red beckon in front. Sihar wakes with a start.

The King ponders the dream for three days and three nights. On the fourth day, Sihar summons his son and daughter before him.

"I have decided," he announces, "to abdicate." Stunned, they stand speechless before their father and their King. He takes the moment to add: "The two of you will rule in my stead, as brother and sister co-sovereigns."

"But why, Father?" Salimar jumps forward. *So like her mother*, Sihar smiles.

"I no longer have the heart to continue," Sihar replies simply, staying his daughter's trembling shoulder with a loving hand. "With your mother's passing, I am now released . . . from my obligation to the Throne. I long to be free to live the rest of my days without councils and decisions . . . so on and so forth." Sihar waves vaguely away the weighty matters of state. He places another hand on Jandar's shoulder. "I was your age when I first ascended to the Throne."

Jandar takes his father's arm firmly and promises: "We will try to do as well as you, Father."

After his children leave, Sihar returns to his inner sanctum. A small chamber off to the side of the immense Throne Hall, this refuge allows the King to contemplate in peace, while fragrant breezes waft in from three sides through the intricately carved rosewood windows. Shedding his sandals, Sihar steps up to the cool, bamboo platform that abuts the south-facing wall. He leans back on the silk pillows behind the massive tree trunk that serves as his place of writing and thinking. Saved from a diseased teak and lacquered with fine oils to smooth its surface, the trunk is covered with scrolls and maps and designs. All sorts of construction are underway, a sign of the Kingdom's prosperity and the King's wise rule. But no work proceeds today. All is in mourning.

Sihar sits as usual. One leg tucks under with the other raised at the knee. His right arm rests on top while his left fingers a pearl rosary. Sihar's thoughts fly back to his first challenge as King. Times were not so peaceful then . . .

Thirty Years Back

"Majesty!" the courier pants with alarm and urgency. "Troops are assembling to our North. The tyrant is invading!"

"Norom of Ashaka!" King Sihar curses under his breath, pounding his fist on the Amber Throne.

Everyone knows of Norom's desire for Vishodhya, his neighbor to the South. Surrounded by sea on three sides, Vishodhya basks in commerce and trade, bounty and contentment; whereas desert parches Ashaka to the North and the East, with mountains blocking it on the West. Only through Vishodhya can Ashaka drink the life-giving circulations of the sea. And precisely for this reliance, seen as a weakness, Norom the Tyrant wants to destroy Vishodhya by conquering it.

The Minister of Rites speaks first.

"Your Majesty." Greybeard bows deeply, his tip almost touching the marble floor. "Let us come to a truce with Norom to prevent war."

King Sihar is young and untried. Just three months on the Amber Throne, he ascended when his beloved grandfather, Boruda, founder of the dynasty, breathed his last. Sihar's own father, as the gods would have it, dissipated youth and promise in the Palace of Pleasures. His sole contribution was to sire a son one moon before collapsing from women and drink. The Court saddens in memoriam but never fails to titter in the hallways, recalling the Prince's salacious escapades . . .

Sihar bears this legacy seriously. He has his father's charm but also his grandfather's astuteness. Sihar relies on both to command the state.

"A notorious tyrant like Norom," Sihar responds, "would never honor a truce. He'd fear we think him weak. Worse yet, he'd fear our neighbors think him weak and that would make him enslave us all."

The Minister of Rites could not disagree. The Minister of War seizes the moment and approaches the Throne, his silver saber rattling eagerly by his side.

"Let us wage war, Majesty, and show them Vishodhya's mettle!"

"War cannot be our first move, Minister," Sihar replies sternly, "only the last. We cannot burden our people with *his* devastations." Boruda had taught his grandson well.

The Minister of War steps back reluctantly. The Minister of Grains now moves forward, humble in the extreme.

"What if," he suggests with the smoothness of a tiger about to pounce, "we starve his people by refusing them water?"

Sihar considers the matter.

"Such a strategy punishes the people, not the tyrant. How would our own respond? They would think us capable of doing the same to them one day. And who could blame them? Once such doubts creep in, how could we rely on them to follow the Throne?" Again, the Minister could not disagree. The King shakes his head slowly. "No, we must think of another way."

But his Ministers are barren of any other thoughts or proposals. Each stands by awkwardly, with hands folded in their long, silk sleeves.

Sihar's eyes rise to the crystal blue sky beyond the Court's marble columns and his heart begins to yearn. He stands up.

"We must clear our head," the King announces. He orders for the royal steed, Duan, one of the famous "sweating blood" horses from the Land of Sand and Figs. Fifteen hands high, Duan is a gift from the Emperor of the Tang to the King of the Amber Throne.

Sihar rides long and hard until he reaches the edge of his Kingdom where a lush, dense forest lies. He likes coming to this forest. It soothes him somehow.

He stops by a brook, letting Duan take in a slow, leisurely drink. The spots on his coat, red when sweating, fade as he cools down. Sihar finds a large rock under a bush and arranges himself comfortably. He closes his eyes. His body and soul welcome the light breeze, the calm shade, even the mindless, endless chatter of crickets . . .

Shenya, the Priestess

A gurgle and a splash interrupt this idyll. Opening his eyes, Sihar turns around to find a woman farther down the brook, wading through the water, coming toward his side of the bank. Covered by bush and rock, he observes her in secret. After reaching, she stands silently with face uplifted and hands folded before an ancient, twisted tree whose thick branches house many a family of birds.

A Priestess, he surmises. Her dress indicates as much. Not a young girl but a grown woman, the Priestess is robed in flowing, white linen tied with three, small knots to one side. *A high Priestess*, Sihar notes with appreciation.

Her coloring and looks suggest a lineage from the Grand Mystic Peaks, famous for their learning and the arts, tea and silk and horses. Two tiny strands of pearls catch Sihar's eye. These encircle her hair, wrapped high atop her head. Otherwise, she is free of the usual vanities of her sex. *No dancing girl nor courtesan is she*, the King judges expertly. Yet Sihar cannot help but admit to her appeal. He watches in quiet admiration her graceful and deliberate movements, made with finely tapered hands and feet. *No false modesty or any other pretense*, he notes. Most interesting are her eyes. Lively and alert, they are, nonetheless, tempered by long-held contemplation.

"Intelligent," the King remarks aloud without realizing it.

"Who's there?" the Priestess demands of the rock and the bush.

Sihar emerges from his sanctuary.

"Pardon, Priestess." He touches his forehead in greeting. "I happened to be resting under this bush . . ." Sihar uses the common "I" instead of the royal "we," hoping to disguise himself. But Shenya recognizes the King of the Amber Throne.

He is tall and lithe, with a thinker's face. Yet he moves with a warrior's grace and agility. Dressed in a simple white cotton tunic for riding, Sihar's muscular legs show to pleasing advantage. A jade-and-ruby locket, strung by thin loops of gold chain, hangs loosely on his chest. Black curls adorn his head. They dance nimbly at the nape of his neck. A royal moustache droops slightly at the ends, covering a mouth that could be, otherwise, too tender. The King's eyes unnerve her slightly. Dark of brow and cast, they are clear and piercing. One suspects they know too much. *Still*, Shenya thinks to herself, *a pleasant young man*, not just *a King*. The thought surprises her. The Priestess folds her hands together with a slight bow.

"Greetings, Your Majesty."

Sihar straightens to his usual royal bearing.

"We greet you, Priestess, and beg your indulgence. What branch of devotion hails you?"

"The Temple of Knowledge, Sire. I study trees."

"Trees?" The King seems slightly amused.

She catches his tone but ignores it. Many respond like this, why less so a King?

"Trees have much to teach us, Sire. Like elephants, they live many lives and store much wisdom within." Talk of the elephant, a sacred animal in his Kingdom, reminds Sihar of his dilemma. The King's spirit sags a little. Shenya notices it and ventures to ask: "What brings my lord to the forest?"

The King doesn't mind the question, so directly posed, usually prohibited by Court protocol. He finds it a relief to talk to this Priestess, at this place, so far from everything and everyone he knows. The King proceeds to tell the Priestess about Vishodhya and Ashaka, war and strategy, the people and his ministers, dilemma and solution . . . so on and so forth. Shenya listens quietly.

"My lord seems dissatisfied with their proposals," she observes, referring to his ministers, after he finishes.

"We need something worthy of us, that will build us up not tear us down!" Sihar declares with more emotion than expected. For some reason, Sihar trusts this Priestess, a mere stranger, just moments ago. He turns to her. "Have you any recommendations?"

Shenya pauses then gestures toward the ancient tree.

"Trees thrive, my lord, when their roots deepen and expand. And they can only do so without blockage by this fence or that, planted by this farmer or that."

"You mean . . . ?"

"Open thy gates, Sire. Ashaka's people are no fools. They will come because they know the tyrant's trick of waging war to distract discontent at home. Once in Vishodhya, they will contribute to thy Kingdom by tilling the land and selling its fruits. Vishodhya's farmers will value the help. And Norom's army will permit this because many of their families are farmers. Once Ashaka is hollowed first of its farmers, then its army, and finally its nobles, Norom will be tyrant over nothing and no one. With him gone, Ashaka's people can return to their homeland. In recompense, Vishodhya's farmers will have first choice in procuring Ashaka's produce but Ashakans can bargain their price. As for Ashaka's nobles, make use of them. They have skills that can only enhance Your Great Benevolence."

A smile slowly overcomes Sihar. This proposal satisfies all his demands: no war, no burden on his people – indeed, just the opposite – and yet Norom is defeated. Brilliant!

Jumping on Duan, he bows elaborately.

"Our thanks, Priestess, 'til next we meet!"

Sihar speeds off. He does not wait for Shenya to respond. He knows they will see each other again.

Royal Decree

Back at Court, King Sihar issues a royal decree. People of Ashaka, it announces, you are welcome! You will receive land and work in Vishodhya, the decree promises, *if* you abandon your sovereign, Norom the Tyrant.

That night, Vishodhya lowers its gates. At first, Ashakans straggle in twos or threes on foot; then whole families come by cattle and carts. Norom's soldiers shut one eye to the exodus. Many of their loved ones are among those leaving. Before long, the soldiers themselves leave. No one wants to lose life or limb, much less family and home, for a vainglorious tyrant. Lastly, the nobles escape, taking with them valuable treasures in silk and jewelry, gold and silver, as well as vital knowledge of Norom's Court.

Norom's reign soon cracks. The tyrant flees and most Ashakans return home to build a new land and a new future. Some Ashakans stay behind. They have found a home and love and family in Vishodhya. Eventually, all Ashakans decide to join with Vishodhyans in territory and rule. After all, Ashakans no longer have a King or Court of their own. And they enjoy working with the Vishodhyans, benefiting from their common labor. Many of Ashaka's soldiers and generals now serve in Vishodhya's army, and their nobles advise King Sihar. Why not issue in name what is practiced in life? Rites and ceremonies are performed. Vishodhyans and Ashakans link hearts and arms in a new era under King Sihar.

Long Live the King! So begins the Kingdom of Vishaka.

The Farmers

But soon, a problem arises. Too much prosperity blights the land! The more the farmers produce, now doubled in size and variety, the more the nobles tax them and often unfairly. "We sweat all day just so they can languish in silks and pearls and wine!" the farmers complain. After downing some of their own (wine, that is), a few former Ashakans grumble that perhaps they had it better under Norom. At least, they knew what they were dealing with! (These grumblings usually give way, next morn, to a painful throbbing in the head.)

King Sihar cannot blame the farmers. With no wars to fight, the nobles – that is, the noble *men* – live lives of wanton leisure, frittering away time on hunting and gaming, song and dance, rarely helping others with their bodies or their minds. Their only activity of note becomes taxation. Many of these nobles are Sihar's kin.

Life for the ladies, Sihar notices, is quite different. Besides bearing and raising children, they manage large households. They are in the kitchen, storing and making food; in the garden, growing vegetables, fruits, herbs, and flowers; in the animal pen, raising chickens, goats, and oxen to harvest their eggs, milk, and meat; in the nurseries, planting the leaves that will feed the worms that will secrete the silk that will be spun, loomed, and woven into the fabric that will be dyed, cut, and stitched into the garments that will clothe each single body. The ladies also attend the market every day to buy, sell, and barter supplies needed for the household.

Of course, the noble ladies do not do everything themselves. They have help. Lower-ranked women, along with maids and other servants, are always on hand to haul, wash, dry, fold, slice, sift, and put things away. Supervising these helpers, the King observes, amounts to another kind of labor.

"What are we to do about the farmers?" Sihar asks Shenya. The King and the Priestess are sitting under the ancient tree by the brook. "They are right to resent the taxes that the nobles claim, enjoying little from their own hard sweat then to be treated like dogs. Yet many of these nobles are from our own royal house. If we upset them, they will challenge our Throne. For this reason," Sihar rues, "we cannot raise this matter at Council."

Shenya listens patiently, then asks: "Are there not other branches to your Giant Palm, Majesty, that give shade and bear fruit, as well as shelter those that live off it?"

"Of course . . ."

"Then why not allow the branches to flourish while leaving the exotic blooms to revel in their own fragrance?"

"Ah . . ." Sihar brightens.

Back at Court, he issues a new order. Ladies, it decrees, you will take charge of the household purse. You may also own and run shops in the market, since you trade in goods daily. Men are too important for such details, the edict adds.

The noblemen nod in solemn agreement. Their wives bow in happy discretion.

The farmers' discontent soon ends. Women, as managers of the household, demand more reasonable taxes. They understand that unfair duties make unhappy farmers who give them poor produce that lead to even unhappier households. The women can afford such graciousness for taxes are no longer their only source of income. Now, they can also buy and sell in the marketplace, enriching their households with goods and trades, wares and products. And who, imagine, becomes their best customers? The farmers and their families! With each passing day, the women and the farmers come to regard each other with greater respect. They know who makes their lives better – and who worse.

Meanwhile, the noblemen care little for taxes or markets or any other matter so long as they can enjoy their pastimes.

Everyone applauds King Sihar's decree. *Long Live the King!* All settle into contentment and routine.

The Young People

But another problem arises. Enjoying peace and prosperity, the people of Vishaka begin to lose a sense of purpose. Life is too easy! People work from dawn 'til dusk during the harvest but that lasts only three moons at most. The rest of the time, they wait for the seeds to grow and strengthen, eventually to poke through the earth. Some women busy themselves with spinning and weaving. But this activity occupies only half a day every other day. What are families – especially the young people – to do in the evenings, before clearing their rush mats for sleep? Many young men begin to imitate the noblemen and pick up frivolous pursuits. Parents *tsk-tsk* on the side but with little effect. Sihar worries his father's ghost may have ascended to the Amber Throne, after all.

"Perhaps," the Minister of Rites suggests, "the young men could engage in competitions to capture their attention, like archery or races or wrestling? With their families cheering on the side, they will feel accomplished."

Sihar considers the proposal quietly.

"How would such competitions give them a sense of purpose?" he inquires. "Would it not make the stronger bully the weaker, the body dismiss the mind? And, as the harvests pass, would not the young and healthy disdain the old and infirm?" Sihar thinks of Shenya. "What of the young women? They have different strengths from their brothers and these are not easily tested by races or wrestling. Would female strengths fall aside as the young men enjoy all the cheer and glory?" Sihar now sees in his mind's eye the giant, black Ancient One that nurtures all with its leaves and branches, principles and wisdom. "What we need, Minister, is to root our people in something strong and everlasting, not subject them to the strife and struggle of constant competition."

The Minister of Rites retreats. He has not considered these points.

"The young ones," the Minister of War declares, "need military discipline! Let us organize them into camps where they must attend to exercises from dawn to dusk. That will instill a sense of purpose in them!"

Sihar has to smile at the Minister's earnestness. He always has the same answer for every problem. And for this problem, Sihar's answer will simply reinforce what he has already said.

Reading the King's expression, the Minister of Grains steps forward agilely.

"How about," he proposes, "we send the young people to the remote countryside and have them labor on unfarmed land? This will not only occupy their bodies but also their minds. And we will gain more farmland and produce. Everyone benefits!"

Sihar takes in a deep breath. Mandu, the Minister of Grains, is a clever fellow but completely lacking in understanding that others may want something quite different from what he desires for himself. Close in age to the Kingdom's young people, Sihar cannot imagine a less inspiring endeavor than farming unfarmed land. But the King still addresses his Minister with courtesy and respect.

"Alas, sending them to the countryside may fulfill *our* sense of purpose more than theirs . . . which may further deprive them of *their* sense of purpose."

Sihar stands up. He knows he must seek counsel elsewhere.

"What to do?" he confides to Shenya, pacing agitatedly by their tree in the forest. He had ridden out early that morn hoping to find her and he did. "People need to enjoy themselves, and they should, but to what end?" He refrains from telling her of the Ministers' proposals and why none satisfies. Besides, he's sure, she already knows.

Shenya considers the King's question carefully. It is more difficult to answer than the first two he posed. Sitting in its shade, she looks up at the giant tree above them. Silently, she beseeches it: *O Ancient One, please guide us with your wisdom.*

As she prays, Shenya cannot help but take in the tree's leaves. They are large and full and green, thick and healthy, despite the heat, the dust, and the bugs, munching solidly away. An orchid flower, perched on an arch between two branches, dimples in the breeze. A beautiful leech of yellow, purple, and red sprays, the orchid graces its ancient and twisted host . . .

Shenya's eyes light up. Sihar leans in attentively. He is beginning to know her ways.

"My lord is right that the people must have their relaxations," she begins. "Build on this natural desire and even leeches can turn into orchids." Sihar's brows rise in puzzlement. Shenya elaborates: "People, like trees, can be grown. The right amount of sun and soil and water are needed, 'tis true, and these will determine how tall and strong the tree will be. But people, like trees, need more than the basic elements to fully flower."

"That is . . . ?" the King prompts.

"They need love."

"Love?" Sihar repeats in surprise. "You mean like – like the feelings between, uh, two *lovers*?" The King clears his throat. Some dust must have flown in.

Shenya smiles kindly. "Yes but love is more than that. Passionate love is important, and we often sing about it or recite poetry when moved by it. But there are other kinds of love as well. There is the love between parents and children, brothers and sisters, teachers and students, and good friends." Shenya notices the King looking away at this point. She continues: "And there is love between

oneself and the Visible, like the Ancient One here –"
Shenya pats the tree in front of her with affection "– and
the Invisible." She holds out her arms, gesturing toward
the Universe. "Both are contained within." She folds back
her arms, resting them on her chest. "Love of oneself is
perhaps the most difficult yet ultimate love."

"Do not the Sages teach that we should forget the self
so as to live well with others?" Sihar probes. "How can
one love oneself, then?"

"The Sages are wise," Shenya replies. "To truly forget
the self, they would agree, one must first know the self.
This requires an internal inquiry: What are our best talents
and our worst lacks? Knowing this, we must also ask:
How can we expand the talents and redress the lacks?
Trees and other life forms have much to teach us on this."
Sihar raises his brows again. Shenya continues: "See this
orchid, Sire?" Shenya points to the arch between the
branches. "At root, this orchid is no more than a leech,
living off the Ancient One. This is the orchid's worst lack.
Yet its ability to survive anywhere, even hanging in air
sometimes, deserves admiration. This is its best talent.
Still, it is the Ancient One that allows the orchid to turn its
lack into a talent. Hosting this orchid is no more or less
burdensome than housing a family of birds. Both help the
Ancient One live a long and happy life. They keep away
those that would bring illness or chew away its innards
until all crumbles into dust. Here, the Ancient One's
grandness – its ability to host many beings – is a talent
and a lack, depending on who visits and for what purpose.

"But more than these rudiments of survival, there is
something else, just as important, that is gained between
the orchid and the tree. That is, beauty and pleasure and
sheer joy. Together, orchid and tree bring forth these
beautiful sprays of color and delicacy for all to enjoy.

"Realizing this, our loneliness ends. We see that we live and breathe, laugh and cry, in a much larger, livelier world than our own small corner of lacks and talents. From such appreciation comes respect. Not one thing, even a lack, is without meaning or purpose. And from respect, love grows. We see that everything and everyone in the Universe can turn a lack into a talent, a seed into a flower, once we find the right conditions and the right friendship." Without knowing why, it is Shenya who looks away this time, her heart beating a little faster than usual. She forces her gaze back to the King: "Thus, we forget the self so as to live well with others."

Sihar strokes his chin.

"So the first step is to know ourselves, to account for our lacks and talents?"

"Yes."

"But no one likes to reveal lacks," Sihar ruminates. "Same with talents. Who desires to appear naked before all to see? Yet these accountings must take place openly. How else could we learn the wisdom of the orchid and the tree?"

As she has so often lately, Shenya finds herself impressed with the King's quick grasp of unfamiliar matters and philosophies even upon first reception.

Sihar starts to pace again.

"But how . . .? That is the question."

"We need to traverse beyond the usual disguises and distractions," Shenya suggests.

"Yes," Sihar agrees. "People must reach into their inner beings."

"Yet they must do so willingly, together with others, like a game . . . or storytelling. They need . . ."

"Dreams!" the King exclaims. Without another word, he whistles for Duan and races back to Court.

Who taught him the power of dreams? Shenya wonders.

Dreams and Other Tales

Another decree quickly comes forth. Once a moon, the edict announces, when there is no harvest, every village from as small as ten families to as many as a hundred, and even the Court itself, will hold an "Evening of Dreams." A drum with a hole pierced in the middle will be placed at a public altar. Within this drum, people will drop a rolled-up sisal scroll. On it will be written or drawn a dream or a wish or a story or anything one would like to tell. At every half-moon, a trusted elder will pick out one sisal scroll from the drum. Young people will perform the selection on the next full moon, the night designated for dreams. All the families will gather round the stage and watch. Afterwards, everyone will discuss the performance.

At first, the "Evening of Dreams" is poorly attended. People are too shy to reveal their innermost thoughts and feelings. Many write funny stories or the pranks they played during the day, like jumping over mushrooms when they should be picking them for dinner. The performances, also, are undertaken with indifference. Young people give their assignment little care or attention.

But one time, a real dream is written on a sisal scroll. It tells of a fantastic, giant bird with flaming orange and purple plumes sweeping down upon a village. The bird's beak opens and out falls a small *sutra.* It lands onto the public altar, glittering with golden thread on a fragment of silk, the color of ripe, dewy pomegranates.

What could this mean?! Everyone wonders and discusses and argues and jokes and jostles and laughs. Some even run to the public altar to see if a golden *sutra* has, indeed, fallen there. They can't wait for the next performance!

The "Evening of Dreams" becomes a most popular event. One performance tells a bittersweet tale of two sweethearts, parted when young by their families who didn't approve, never to see each other again. Many harvests pass and the man's beard grows white. One night, he sees the woman again in a dream. She is as he knew her, with big, bright eyes and long, black, shiny hair. "Hello again," the vision smiles, then it is gone. A year later, word comes from a relative that she died that night.

There is little discussion after this performance. The women drop quiet tears, while the men pull on their pipes thoughtfully. From that day on, Sihar notices, people are more courteous, much gentler with one another.

Another performance tells of a daughter-in-law who is poorly treated by her demanding mother-in-law. The daughter-in-law is so miserable she dreams of hanging herself with a strand of gleaming, white silk.

Much talk follows this performance. Daughters-in-law form a group to help one another with their chores, so a demanding mother-in-law could be satisfied. Mothers-in-law also form a group to make sure no one could be so demanding!

Even the noblemen become affected. One performance tells of water. Women sometimes walk half a day to carry two heavy, swishy barrels of water, linked by a pole, on their thin, straining shoulders. A dream comes to a young servant girl, after an exhausting day of hauling water. In it, she sees water flowing through bamboo pipes into a central well. But it is just a dream. And she is just a servant girl.

The King's cousin is deeply moved by this dream. He sets about tying one bamboo pipe after the other, just like in the dream. Soon, the springs are rushing through the bamboo pipes. Women are able to fetch water whenever and however they like. Their shoulders no longer ache and bruise from the unforgiving poles. In time, the well becomes more than a well. It beckons men and women, young and old, to come and eat, drink, joke, banter, and flirt. Everyone looks to the well for fun and activity, news and gossip, as soon as the sun rises until it sets. Even then, many often gather by with candles and fermented drinks to swap tales, sing songs, and simply gaze at the luminous stars above.

The well inspires other young noblemen to help in other ways. Somehow, spending all their time hunting or gaming or pursuing leisure no longer seems so satisfying.

The children now want performances of their own. They see how much their parents and the other big people enjoy them. The children persist so much their parents finally give in. Soon, the children's performances grow in number. Some make the parents smile as the children stage tricks or put on plays. Others give unexpected lessons. In one, a little girl happily shows her mother a drawing of a flower, only to have the mother say, "The stem isn't straight enough" or "the petals are crooked." The little girl hides under a coconut palm, crying. Another performance shows a little boy suffering the taunts of a bigger boy, only to have his father laugh at him for being taunted. The little boy finds an over-ripe watermelon and stomps it to pieces.

After these performances, every parent becomes quiet. That evening, before bed, parents hug their children just a little longer than usual.

Word spreads of these magical evenings. Many come from afar to witness them or have their own dreams performed and discussed. Sometimes visiting pilgrims are invited to share their knowledge of the wider world. One who comes from climes hotter than Vishaka's spellbind young and old alike with his tales of wondrous places and their even more wondrous inhabitants. There is a man and a bird, the pilgrim recites in his singsong voice, who help each other survive in a land so burnt and dry it cracks the soil and singes the feet. The man protects the bird from predators, while the bird helps the man distract bees from their hive so he can steal the golden, delicious nectar within. "Oooohhh!" the audience amazes out loud.

The King finds himself turning to the Priestess more and more. Each one of her counsels benefits the Kingdom and its people greatly. But he can find Shenya by chance only. Once, he rode to the forest three times and back over two days with none but the brook, the trees, the animals, and the flowers to bear witness.

"Come to Court," the King urges the Priestess, the last time they meet in the forest. "Vishaka needs you." *I need you*, Sihar concedes privately.

"Alas, Sire, I must decline." Shenya lowers her eyes. "I gladly serve Your Majesty but my devotion, the Temple, believes that knowledge requires removal from the mundane world."

Sihar knows he has to appeal directly to the only person who can persuade Shenya to leave: the Abbess of the Temple of Knowledge.

The Abbess

The Abbess of the Temple of Knowledge is a woman of extraordinary age and accomplishment. It is said that she studied with the First Pilgrims. Though shriveled and bent, she remains clear-eyed and sharp-minded.

The Abbess receives the King in the Hall of Great Learning, a chamber of cool marble and tall columns scented by ever-burning incense. Though grand and imposing, the Hall of Great Learning truly impresses with its aura of tranquil and timeless wisdom.

The Abbess and the King sit, side by side, on pillows of raw silk. Before them is a short tray of lacquered vermilion inlaid with silver clouds, upheld by four lion legs, a present from another sovereign. On the tray are two tiny cups of tea in exquisite, almost translucent, white porcelain. Beside these are small dishes of dates, nuts, and dried fruits.

"Perhaps an exception could be made?" the King persists, referring to Shenya.

The Abbess returns the King's smile with a slight bow.

"Our Temple, Sire, has rules just as thy Kingdom has rules." The Abbess looks down to smooth the folds of her already immaculately folded robe, a habit developed from an eternity of dealing with sovereigns.

The King remains resolute.

"Surely, Learned One, you recognize Priestess Shenya's importance for Vishaka."

"We love this land and its people as much as Your Majesty," the Abbess replies with the utmost delicacy, "but we respond to a calling that is no less inferior."

The King makes one more appeal.

"Your Temple is known far and wide for its learning and devotion, Abbess. Please accept this small token of our appreciation."

King Sihar claps his hands twice. Twelve tall and burly men enter, two-by-two, each pair carrying a large, round plate of burnished bronze. Rare gifts pile high on each: bolts of *shoo* brocade from the land of bears and mulberry; black tea compressed into flat wheels, each the size of a man's outstretched hands when placed side-by-side; poles of *perra* bamboo, the best for construction of any kind; precious spices like cinnamon, peppercorns, ginger, turmeric, and salt; precious metals like tin, lead, copper, gold, and silver; and lastly, incense from the temples of Dali, Bagan, Pyè, and Assam. A King's ransom, indeed!

The Abbess scarcely gives them a glance. Her eyes stare straight ahead even as her words address the King directly.

"Surely, Sire, thou canst think so little of this Temple."

Sihar sighs inwardly. He should have known mere *things* would not impress the Abbess. Her Temple is not to be bribed of a Priestess!

The King signals to leave. To bargain further would demean them both. He will have to take his chances on finding Shenya in the forest.

The Abbess escorts the King outside, where Duan and the rest of the Royal Guards await. Just as Sihar mounts his steed, the jade-and-ruby locket around his neck, worn always near his heart, taps lightly against his skin, cooling it. A habit since childhood, the King's left hand traces the contours of his pendant, while his right holds Duan's tasseled reins. For several moments, Sihar seems lost in thought.

The Abbess waits patiently by the Temple's gate. She would not presume to imagine what delays His Majesty. The Royal Guards move nary an inch but their steeds start to chomp and stomp. *What's going on?* they neigh to each other. But Duan calmly swishes his tail and sniffs at a beetle bug scurrying from his nose. Duan senses his master's contemplation. *We can wait.*

"Our apologies, Learned One, if we have offended." The King dismounts in one swift motion and returns to the Abbess.

Surprised, the Abbess is, nonetheless, too elevated to reveal it. She bows again slightly. "None taken, Your Majesty."

"You are most gracious but please allow us a redemption," Sihar insists. He lifts his locket and opens it to extract a small, folded fragment of silk, the color of faded pomegranates, threaded in gold.

This time, the Abbess cannot contain her surprise. Imperceptibly, she draws in a breath.

"This *mantra*," Sihar explains, "was given to us when a young boy. A laughing monk in beggar's clothes was passing through and gave it to us. 'This *mantra* will save your life one day,' he said. 'All you have to do is show it.' We have often been tempted to use it, especially in battle –" the young King gazes at the *mantra* fondly "– but never could we part with it . . . 'til now." He offers the *mantra* to the Abbess respectfully, with both hands.

She receives it from the King, also with both hands. The Abbess recognizes the *mantra* immediately. It reminds her of someone from long ago and far away . . .

"We will bear Shenya's absence with much fortitude." The Abbess bows to the King.

At Court

And so Shenya is installed at Court. It consists of one, immense garden, filled with greenery and fragrance, butterflies and peacocks, and, of course, turtles and ponds and unfolding lily pads. One garden enters into another and another and another. Each one houses the Court's ministers, courtiers, and other servants, starting with the lowest ranked. (Sihar places Shenya in a small compound, one garden removed from his.) One can walk for half a day from one garden to the next until, finally, one reaches the only garden left in the center and that is, of course, the Royal Palace.

A golden structure of teak and marble, the Palace curves around several inner courtyards. Each corner of the compound is open to the others, in part to emphasize the Royal Benevolence, but also to shield the King from invaders. The lower chambers conduct the Kingdom's business; the upper ones house the King and his family. One uninterrupted terrace winds around the upper quarters, overlooking the massive, linked gardens. The upper levels of the Palace also provide guestrooms for visiting dignitaries.

A tiny kiosk pinnacles on top. It looks down at the tallest palms, where cooling breezes greet the guard always on duty. Exquisitely carved friezes line the palace walls on the outside. These tell of gods and goddesses, kings and consorts, generals and nymphs, farmers and laborers, each a reminder of Vishaka's glory – past, present, and future.

Inside, all is lightness and air. Each room delights in width and height; its screen-like walls embroidered with moons, stars, flowers, birds, and other designs to welcome the breeze, whenever and wherever it may blow. Above, intricate weaves of sisal sealed with fragrant oils of palm and sandalwood keep out the rain, the bugs, and other possible visitors. Yet the sisal breathes, filling the rooms with cooling drafts. Thickets of bamboo with their green, sprouting leaves mixed with blossoming white jasmine and pink camellias accompany stairways of running water, gurgling over ebony pebbles. Pairings of such "flowering bamboo and flowing water" cover the length of the Palace hallways, relieving the heat and the dust with a beauty that intoxicates the eye, the nose, the ear, not to mention the heart. *A paradise within*, Shenya admires when first entering the Palace.

The grandness of Court does not affect her. Shenya continues to go about in her simple, priestly robes and eat only the plainest foods. Still, she enjoys the plenty and the pageantry at Court. Even the lowest-ranked maids, her keen eye notes, go about in graceful silks of every color and cut, fresh even in the midday sun.

Shenya meets with the King daily at dawn in Council, along with the other Ministers. Soon enough, Sihar notices that Shenya often gives the best, most comprehensive, and workable proposals. She does so not by competing against the Ministers, nor by pitting one against the other, but by drawing them together, composing a whole from the various parts. *Subtle*, the King admires.

Rest of the day, Shenya continues to study trees. She wants to learn how Vishaka's native grown could multiply with fruits and flowers brought from elsewhere. Gifts of such sometimes come as a tribute of goodwill from an ambassador on behalf of his King or lord. Other times, a pilgrim or a merchant would pass through bringing along a rare treasure. Still other times, an item finds its way to market. Shenya gathers all the varieties she encounters, brings them back to the Palace, and prays to them in her nursery, seeking their wisdom and consent, before gently twining one exotic to a local. She packs them in cool mud to ease their growth, and adds a layer of wild *arum* leaves to shelter them from the burning sun. She makes sure to leave a little opening in the south-facing chamber so the entwined fates can breathe fully and easily. On wet, cool nights, she covers them with branches of the *jujube* tree, so their active life-force can blanket the tiny seedlings forming within. In time, a third being peeks through the rich, black earth, ready to spring forth with color and fragrance, blossom or fruit.

"Would they grow in such delicate settings only?" Sihar asks when he visits her in the nursery one day. It is a large, open area, shaded by an awning of palm leaves, in front of the chamber where she sleeps. A short curtain of mother-o'-pearl divides the two spaces.

"I hope to help them thrive in all climes, Sire," Shenya answers.

The King nods with approval. (At moments like these, he cannot help but admire the graceful curve of Shenya's neck or the melody of her voice or how her hands bend and flow like river reeds when describing something avidly . . .)

"Why do you trouble with such?" he asks again, trying to stay his wandering mind.

"This one, Sire –" Shenya points to a bunch of yellow and orange sprouts "– will perfume a whole garden with one bud." She turns to the next pot, full of green shoots with purple spots. "This one will bear the juiciest, reddest berries but hungry bugs will eat only the leaves, not the fruit." She comes to a large, round bamboo basket, squatting next to the mother-o'-pearl curtain, filled with seeds the color of dried mud. "And this one, Sire, will help the others grow tall and strong."

"Like the Ancient One," the King smiles. (*And what a charming smile it is!* The observation catches Shenya off-guard. She waves away an imaginary fly. *Don't be silly*, she chastises herself.)

By dusk, the Priestess is no longer on duty. Yet she often finds herself in the King's company – this time as he eases from the day's demands. They would dine at a terrace by his favorite lotus pond surrounded by blossoms and blooms, peacocks and parrots. Court musicians would pluck on their reedy instruments, floating magic in the air. After dinner, Sihar and Shenya would walk on the stone bridge that arches over the pond bathed in moonglow. Often, in the course of conversation, with a clever word or a gesture or simply a look, Shenya would make the King laugh. So deep and full would his merriment be that it would resound throughout the terrace, startling the frogs, flushing the doves, filling the pond with slippery, silvery rings. And the massive, magnolia trees would sigh with delight.

The Plot

But not all is pleased. Two, in particular, want to rid the King of the Priestess. One is the Minister of Grains, Mandu, a man of mean and envious temperament. The other is Urma, his beautiful but conniving daughter. Father and daughter seek to ascend to the Amber Throne by marrying Urma to Sihar. As Royal Consort, Urma would greatly advance her family, especially since the Kingdom has doubled in size and treasure. However, it is also clear to Mandu and Urma, plain as the crow flies, that Sihar has eyes for none other than Shenya. And so they begin to plot.

Mandu discovers that the tyrant Norom has retreated to the mountains in the West. Deposed, Norom has nowhere else to go. Mandu sends word through spies. *If you seek your Kingdom's return*, he writes on a sisal scroll curled in a courier's belt, *you need Sihar's secret. We can deliver her.*

Norom replies with one word: *Proceed*.

Next afternoon, during that peaceful lull when all nap after the noonday meal, Urma sneaks into Shenya's quarters. The Priestess is resting quietly on her mat.

"Awake, Sister Priestess!" Urma rouses Shenya with hurried whispers. "His Majesty needs you!"

Shenya rises immediately. "What's happened?"

"His Majesty fainted on his horse outside the city gate. He wants no one to know. Come quickly!"

Distressed, Shenya does not notice Urma's nervous eyes or flushing cheeks. Shenya simply jumps into Urma's chariot and speeds with her to the city's northern gate, far from the Royal Palace.

Once there, Shenya quickly senses something amiss. The Royal Guards are nowhere about. They always accompany His Majesty wherever he goes. Instead, soldiers in unfamiliar colors emerge from behind the bushes and the trees. They are from another royal house . . . Norom! The tyrant grabs Shenya by the arm and drags her out of Urma's chariot.

"You are mine now, Priestess!" he menaces, a red vein bulging angrily above his right eye.

Shenya faces her nemesis. "Such treachery unbecomes you, Lady Urma."

"What care I," Urma laughs, her face ablaze with triumph, "when I rule from the Amber Throne as Sihar's Queen!" With a crack of the whip amidst a cloud of dust, Urma races off in her chariot, back to Court.

What a woman! Norom's heart beats wildly, much to his surprise.

Rumors flood the Court. There seems no evidence of transgression. Who would dare? *Perhaps she returned to the learned life*, some whisper as the King passes by. Others trade in malicious gossip. *A nobleman has roused her fancy and she's run away with him!*

Sihar knows better. Shenya would never betray him. His emissaries confirm she has not returned to the Temple of Knowledge. Urma seizes the opportunity to comfort the King.

"Try these wines," she suggests, in the guise of consolation. "Sample these delicacies."

But Sihar cannot take to such fancies. He must think. Night after night, he stands alone on the bridge overlooking the lotus pond.

Where are you? the King calls out to the stars.

In Captivity

Norom blindfolds Shenya before swinging her behind him as they ride hard and fast to parts unknown. Still, she can tell where they are headed. A certain crispness cuts through the air, and the fragrance of local plants suggests mountains and lakes. *They must be heading West*, she deduces.

Endless days and endless nights swirl by. Finally, they reach Norom's hideout. The tyrant jumps off his horse and barks an order to someone nearby. Shenya can't hear quite what since the blindfold covers her ears. She feels someone reach for her hands, helping her dismount. He leads her inside, away from the cutting cold. She regrets not her long hair blows hither and thither, the pearl strands lost somewhere along the way. At least she feels warmer this way. Norom's underling lights a torch hanging from a pole inside the cave, then gently unties Shenya's blindfold.

Blinking and rubbing her eyes, Shenya quickly adjusts to the new light and her new surroundings. She is in a dark, dank cave. But it is fit for human living. A rough blanket lies atop a bed of dry leaves in one corner. In the middle of the cave squats a black iron pot with a ladle hooked on the side. (*How? Where?* Shenya wonders. Iron is too precious and too heavy a metal for these parts. *He must have help*, she guesses.) Under the pot are three blackened stones where the underling builds a fire with the torch. Earthen jars of different sizes and shapes line the cave's wall. Some are filled with rainwater; others, dried fruits and nuts. Several bowls stacked one inside the other accompany the iron pot, waiting for their different uses. *This must be the cooking and storage center for the camp*, Shenya guesses again.

Covering the cave's threshold is a curtain of thick, thatched bamboo. It secures the prisoner while also helping to withstand nights of howling wind and stormy rain. Clumps of straw mixed with mountain herbs are strewn on the hard-rock ground to discourage rats, bats, and other potential cohabitants.

Norom's underling presents Shenya with a coat of dried goatskin. The mountain air requires it, so different from Vishaka's lush warmth . . .

The underling avoids Shenya's eyes. He fears women who know too much. *They make bad wives*, his father had warned when he was a boy. No explanation followed but the caution stuck. Women, the father drummed into the son, should be treated like herd animals: all body and no mind.

When the underling raises the curtain to leave, Shenya sees two armed guards standing at attention outside the cave. Long, sharp sabers glint by their sides, next to hungry, snarling dogs. No one can come in or go out easily.

Shenya collapses on the blanket over the bed of leaves. She will need all her wits to deal with Norom in the days ahead.

Talking Fishes

Sleep evades Sihar as he stands on that stone bridge. A full moon has passed and still no word of Shenya. Not even the common folk have any clues to report. Sihar looks up at the sparkling sky. Suddenly, he remembers Shenya's prayer whenever she feels at a loss. Silently and naturally, the words come forth: *O Ancient One, please guide us with your wisdom*. But the Ancient One is in the forest, far away. Sihar has nowhere to turn except downwards to the water in the lotus pond. There, he sees the pond's many goldfish, waving their filmy fins to gaze up at him, mouths opening and shutting, as if trying to say something . . .

Sihar straightens up. A vision flashes before his eyes. The goldfish and their wordless mouths remind him of the last time he visited Shenya at her nursery, shortly before she disappeared.

* * *

That day, Shenya showed him a handful of seeds, scooped from the large basket under the mother-o'-pearl curtain.

"I plant these seeds into the ground," she told him, "to see if they will flourish into fine flowers and fruits in our clime."

And she showed him how. She dug several small holes in the ground and watered them until they turned into black, moist beds of soil. Then she dropped the seeds in, as though feeding pellets of grain into the gaping mouths of fish . . .

* * *

Sihar runs to Shenya's nursery. Sealed from prying eyes and prattling tongues, it is just as she had left it. Standing there now, at the nursery's entrance, he finds seeds scattered on the ground, forming a crooked line from the basket near her chamber to outside the nursery, like a battalion of drunken ants fallen asleep in their tracks. A dent inside the basket tells of a hasty scoop on the way out. *Why was I so blind?* the King curses himself.

Just then, a warm breeze caresses Sihar on the cheek. It bears an unusually strong and sweet bouquet. *This one, Sire, will perfume a whole garden with one bud . . .* Sihar breathes in deeply. The fragrance comes from the West.

"Guards!" the King calls out, and all rush toward him. "Prepare the horses!"

Shenya's Retreat

Shenya wakes early next morn. She peers through a hole in the thatched curtain and sees that the two guards have slumped into slumber, much against their master's orders. But the dogs are up and alert. They menace with a low and steady growl, baring teeth capable of ripping a grown man apart with a single swipe. Soon they, too, lie down in repose. A sprinkling of herbs has settled on their snouts, blown through the curtain's hole. At first, the dogs sneeze. Then they y-a-w-n and s-t-r-e-t-c-h. Finally, they can resist no longer and lie down, closing their eyes and yelping to happy frolics of puppy fun.

Shenya puts the herbs back in the pouch inside her gown, along with other assorted seeds gathered from various wanderings in fields and forests, rivers and streams. One never knows, she believes, when their usefulness comes.

Shenya tries to see as much as she can through the hole in the curtain. Indeed, they are high in the mountains. The terrain is hard and jagged. *A steep climb*, she judges.

Before her are Norom's troops, still huddled on the ground. Each group of five circles a smoldering fire. She counts twenty. Not a large gathering, she thinks, but more might be stationed elsewhere. Besides, these are the most hardened of Norom's men. With no family to return to nor land to till, they have no one but the tyrant. For this reason, they are still with him. And for this reason, they are more dangerous than ten times their number.

Shenya sees that their horses are corralled in a pen off to one side. Its latch is loose. A horse could easily amble out. She has a way of whistling to any animal to come to her, naturally and willingly. The horse could pick its way gingerly between the snoring bodies on the ground, not waking a soul. But escape might bring more harm than good. Norom would punish his guards for losing her. He might try to smoke her out, also, by setting fire to the trees and the bushes. *No*, she decides, *I will need Sihar's troops to bring Norom and his men to justice*. She retreats back into the cave.

The earth thunders and quakes as Sihar and his men charge to the mountains in the West. Sihar knows instinctively that Shenya had dropped the seeds that would perfume a whole garden with one bud. Her yellow and orange sprouts, now flush throughout the mountains, wave him onward. Making camp that night, Sihar encounters an unexpected source of encouragement. Looking down, he finds fat, happy bugs trailing one after the other in a complacent stroll. They lead Sihar to green bushes with purple spots bursting with juicy, red berries. Only the leaves are eaten, not the fruit. Sihar's men benefit from this boon of refreshment. But the berries also point to a path deeper and higher into the mountains. And toward this destination Sihar and his men ride, then climb, for the next fortnight.

Norom's Demand

"I want you to advise me as you have King Sihar!" Norom barks to Shenya that night. "I want my Kingdom back!"

Norom is drunk with victory and wine. The red vein over his eye bulges bigger than ever. Shenya eyes it with concern. He had staggered into her cave, one hand clutching a gourd of wine, the other gesturing wildly before her. He expects her to cower and beg for mercy. Instead, Shenya regards him with sadness. Sensing her charity, Norom spirals further into rage and lurches at her lasciviously.

"But first, woman, let me give you a taste of what it means to be with a *real* man!"

"If thou willst violate my body, Sire," Shenya replies coolly, "thou willst destroy my mind. How can I advise thee, then?"

The bracing formality of Shenya's speech checks Norom cold. He steadies himself.

The underling keeps his head down but casts a sideways glance at the Priestess. He can't believe her audacity. *She must be mad.*

"Make sure you're ready, Priestess or Witch or Whatever-You-Are," Norom slurs while taking another swig of wine. "For I will see you in the morrow." He stumbles out and Shenya sinks gratefully by the fire under the iron pot.

Shenya's Counsels

True to his word, Norom returns next day at sunset.

"I want my counsel now, Priestess!" he orders and reclines onto a short, wooden bench. The underling places before Norom a small table of folded bamboo, typical of military campaigns that require light, easy-to-carry fixtures. On top of the table, the underling sets a large clay bowl of wild fowl cooked in prunes, mangoes, nuts, and – a special treat – juicy, red berries. Shenya's eyes catch them on the side, though she is careful not to betray her interest. *The seeds must be growing faster in this mountain clime*, she notes. A gourd of wine appears, of course. Next, the underling puts on the table a surprisingly delicate, small blue-and-white porcelain bowl filled with lemon juice and jasmine petals. It reminds her of similar bowls from her ancestors from the Grand Mystic Peaks . . .

Norom dips his fingers in the bowl before tearing into his meal. The underling stands by, ready to service his master with a napkin of white muslin folded over one arm.

Shenya admires the meal less so for its sumptuousness than its inventiveness, especially under such challenging circumstances. *Does Norom appreciate such artistry?* she wonders. Shenya observes that the tyrant consumes his fowl in the customary fashion, with right thumb and first two fingers. Yet his manner, though correct, reveals an innate recklessness. *So different from . . .* She quickly rouses herself to the task at hand.

"What does Your Majesty seek to know?" Shenya inquires.

"How we can regain our Kingdom!" Norom resumes the royal "we." He had lost that will until now.

Shenya pauses, then says: "A fallen tree must upright its stem."

"What?!" Norom sputters.

"Nurture thy roots, Sire."

"What are you talking about?!" Norom shouts. "Stems? Roots? Nurture? Make sense, woman!"

Shenya is not deterred. She picks up the iron ladle from its hook and makes as if to dig the ground to demonstrate.

"Plant thy roots in rich soil, Sire, and –"

But Norom screams her short.

"*Enough of this tree talk!*"

Rage swells his face, whitening his eyes. The vein on his forehead pulses faster and larger, now purpling into an angry scar. Norom jumps from his seat but falls forward, overturning the table and all its contents. The blue-and-white finger bowl shatters into pieces, piercing the air with pain and urgency.

Norom's body twists and jerks like a hapless fish on land. His eyes fall deeply into their sockets. White foam bubbles rudely from his mouth. Shenya quickly reaches for Norom to buffer his head with her lap. His head, already bruised, no longer bangs against the ground. Holding him thus, Shenya knows, also protects his tongue. It seems unmoored but risks not being swallowed.

Norom's underling knows not what to do. He cannot speak, cannot move. He has never witnessed anything like this before. Certainly, not in his lord and master.

"Check the guards," Shenya directs in a low but calm voice.

The underling sneaks a look at the guards through the thatched curtain. They have not detected anything. They are used to the tyrant's tirades.

"Evil spirits?" the underling whispers.

"No," Shenya replies. "Fire has inflamed his body. Once doused, it will no longer harm him. But no one must know."

The underling nods. They both intuit that, if Norom's men get wind of his incapacity, they will mutiny and burn the camp down before dispersing. The men would also kill them without hesitation. A half-dead King, an underling, and a hostage are all unnecessary burdens.

"Tell everyone His Majesty is spending the night with me," Shenya instructs. "Then come back at daybreak with a few of his comforts. I will also need you to gather some herbs."

The underling nods again and slips out the cave.

Maybe the Old Man was wrong, he reconsiders.

The Secret

That night after his body stops trembling, Shenya wraps Norom in the goatskin coat and fans the fire into leaping flames. She makes sure to keep Norom warm despite the sweat flooding his brow. She also brews a special tea with her herbs in the iron pot. She ladles some into the smallest bowl and holds it to his lips to drink, even a little bit, despite the trickles down his chin and neck. She quickly dries them with the muslin napkin. Shenya nurses Norom through the night, all the while silencing her own fatigue.

When dawn peeks through the thousand points of weave in the cave's thatched curtain, Shenya eases a little. The immediate danger is past. The tyrant is breathing more easily in his sleep.

The underling returns at the agreed hour. Much to his relief, he finds his master resting quietly on the bed of leaves. The underling brings over the silk bedding and other royal comforts, and arranges them quickly and capably around the tyrant.

"How should I address you?" Shenya asks, interrupting his servitude.

"I – I have always been called Underling, Priestess," he stammers.

Shenya pauses in her work.

"How did your parents call you?"

"Uh, Twelve. I was the last of the brood," he answers humbly.

Shenya regards him thoughtfully, then asks again: "Were you the one who made the feast last night?"

The underling dips his head shyly.

"It wasn't quite a feast, Priestess, merely a bowl of –"

"Artistry!" Shenya exclaims.

The underling cannot believe his ears. Such high praise from a High Priestess! No one, not even his mother, has given him so much.

"I – I have always thought of food-making as a kind of art," he admits.

"Shall we call you Tandra, then? For 'artist' is what you are!"

The underling beams from his soul.

"If – if you say so, Priestess."

"So be it, Tandra!" The Priestess and the underling smile at each other and forge an eternal bond. "Now," Shenya returns to the matter before them, "please, gather these ingredients. I believe they are particular to this region."

She gives him a list: white fungus grown only on trees that thrive in the shade; yellow wildflowers from the southern, not northern or eastern or western, side of a hill; black, dry bark and tender, green grass from the banks of fresh springs; and a handful of earthworms along with two scorpions, key to Norom's recovery. Meanwhile, an ashen-faced Norom lies prostrate, unaware of the world and the world of him.

They work silently and furiously. Tandra brings back the ingredients that afternoon and helps Shenya cut, chop, and grind them into powder, stirred into Norom's tea. Tandra supports Norom's head and shoulders while Shenya feeds him the reviving brew, spoon by spoon.

Days pass but Norom's men do not miss him. They accept that their lord and master is preoccupied with the Priestess. After all, they wink and nudge, he is a man and she his prisoner! As rough men, they do not question why he spends all day and all night in the cooking and storage cave rather than his own, more decorous tent.

They also welcome the respite. Far from home, they grudgingly take this mountain hideout as a temporary haven, even if remote, rugged, and bare.

The Recovery

Shenya prepares certain foods to help Norom recover, with Tandra an eager accomplice. There is something about the Priestess, he discovers, that differs from anyone he has ever known. It could be that she always speaks to him with courtesy and respect, sharing her knowledge of herbs and medicines and how they match with certain foods. Or it could be her calm and generous presence. Whatever it is, he decides, he is grateful for it.

To deflect suspicion, Shenya and Tandra make the same food for the men as for Norom. They smoke carp over cypress wood, simmer wild boar in wine, and *satay* dove meat on a stick. Duck eggs, turtle eggs, even peacock eggs enter the mix. Chestnuts, walnuts, pine nuts, peanuts – all *kinds* of nuts – accompany these repasts along with a variety of mushroom, fungus, lake weed, and roots.

The mountains brim with fruits like bananas, mangoes, jackfruit, durian, papaya, pommelo, pineapple, rambutan, guava, and avocado, just to name a few. Each finds its way into a meal or a drink. Tandra discovers a rare field of sugarcane nearby. With the cane juice, they are able to balance the bitter with the sweet, the salty with the sour. Shenya also helps Tandra knead the flour he brought to camp and pound them into flatbreads that they bake by sticking them to the inside hull of the iron pot. A few are burned at first but, in time and with practice, each flatbread comes out hot, crunchy, and delicious. And she brews heady teas for the morning; lighter ones for the afternoon.

The meals take effect. They soothe the nerves, heal injuries, regulate the bowels, and strengthen sleep. For men who have survived on snake or mice or any other vermin they could catch for the moment, wherever they are, roughly roasted over an open fire, without salts or spices or any other kind of flavoring, they suddenly find themselves in paradise.

Many offer to help Tandra forage for the ingredients needed for their meals. They sense instinctively that the Priestess is responsible for their sudden good fortune. They haven't seen their lord and master in a while, but none wants to forgo the delicious eating for sight of the tyrant.

Besides, with better sleep and digestion, the men become less warlike. They start taking better care of their horses and dogs, washing and brushing their coats until they shine, even at night. The dogs, in particular, no longer scratch at matted, sunken bellies. Better fed and better loved, they wag happy tails with lolling tongues, more prone to napping and playing than snarling or fighting.

Some of the men start to sing after dinner. Others join in. They begin with well-known campaign songs of battles ancient and mythical. A few recall ditties from boyhoods full of family and home. As the evening wears on, snatches of love and youth and other tender melodies take over. The men's voices wobble at first, a shy trickle despite their rough and mannish source, then they gather force like a mighty waterfall, rolling thunderously to the end. The men *hurrah* and slap one another on the back, congratulating themselves on a life well led!

Back at Court

Before departing the Palace, Sihar puts Greybeard, the Minister of Rites, in charge. Mandu and Urma are secretly delighted. They regard Greybeard as old and feeble, easy to manipulate. Father and daughter spare no effort to flatter the Minister. They invite him to sumptuous meals and present him with precious gifts. Urma befriends his wives, his daughters, even his granddaughters. Mandu seeks Greybeard's advice on matters large and small, making sure to wax eloquently on the Minister's wisdom, foresight, courage, and dedication.

"He lies in the palm of our hands!" father and daughter crow, deep into the night, when others pursue more peaceful dreams.

They fail to notice that the Minister keeps his own counsel. There is reason for Sihar's trust. In his youth, Greybeard had served Sihar's grandfather. They founded the dynasty together. Greybeard is not about to let it go to a pair of conniving upstarts.

The Minister develops an efficient courier system, with stations established at every half-day runs. In this way, couriers can replenish horses and supplies to continue indefinitely. No part of the Kingdom is beyond reach. Sihar has been away for almost two moons, rushing ever faster toward the mountains and away from his capital. Yet he is kept informed of all developments at Court. Greybeard makes sure of that.

Urma's Ambition

More than her father, Urma lives for her ambitions. A woman of exceptional, sometimes too quick, intelligence, Urma is dedicated to escaping a fate common to royal beauties. A fate, that is, like her mother's.

Plucked from her family at fifteen to marry Mandu, a man almost twice her age, Urma's mother was valued for her quiescent loveliness only. She gave birth after birth of disappointing girl babies who survived, of which Urma was the first, or boy babies who fell ill and died when still infants. When Urma's mother was spent of her womb, Mandu took another bride, a woman of younger beauty and fertility. Urma's mother cried for days and refused to eat. Still, Mandu would not give up his concubine. Finally, on a cool Spring night, just before harvest, when all slept soundly under a big, round moon, Urma's mother downed two vials of rat poison and ended her life.

Urma never forgave her father but neither did she let him know it. She knew she needed him to succeed. Only with greater power, Urma felt sure, could she protect herself. Unlike her mother, whom she loved but thought weak, Urma believed in herself. She accepted that men ruled the world but nothing decreed she could not rule *them*. No man would do to her, Urma vowed, what her father did to her mother.

For his part, Mandu never did beget a son. The second wife turned out incapable of carrying his seed. Time and again a bloody and painful mess would disturb the whole household, his concubine crying pitifully in her old nanny's arms. Eventually, Mandu sent both to a remote village to rest – forever.

Mandu's third consort fared no better. She was not interested in sharing a moment, much less a bed, with her illustrious husband. And Mandu, by then, was too old to insist.

He took comfort in his eldest. She seemed to have inherited his drive and intelligence. He may have an heir, after all. *Never mind*, Mandu consoled himself, *even if she is a girl*.

Plots Upon Plots

Urma continues to scheme. If Sihar were to come back triumphant, she calculates, they would be exposed as

Norom's accomplices. Sihar would have every reason to execute them or, worse, banish them to the wilds. If, however, Norom were triumphant, he might reward her and her father – but not too much. Even if she could convince Norom to take her as Queen, he might fear her presence at Court. After all, she belongs to the defeated royal house. Norom would hide her away, at best, to shield her from the wrath of Sihar's loyalists or, at worst, to erase her memory and how he came to the Amber Throne.

No, Urma tightens her delicate hands into iron fists. She will bow to no one! She *will* be Queen. That is her destiny.

I need something more, Urma decides. Something that no one would expect yet would benefit her greatly. She ponders long and hard. One evening, while fanning herself on a hot, heavy night, pregnant with monsoon, an idea bursts upon her just as the skies clatter with refreshing rain. She will ally with her conspirator's conspirators!

During their negotiations on Shenya's kidnapping, Norom revealed a secret. Three Kings, neighbors to Sihar, promised soldiers and supplies to Norom should he invade Vishaka. As a token of their goodwill, they sent Norom a rare iron pot with ladle to aid him during exile. They added an exquisite blue-and-white porcelain bowl from the Grand Mystic Peaks as a gesture of *noblesse oblige*. It served to remind Norom who had the power *and* the Throne.

The Three Kings made this secret pact with Norom out of fear and hope. In King Sihar's presence, they congratulated him for excellent relations as a neighbor, started from his grandfather's time. But privately, amongst themselves, the Three Kings feared Vishaka's new growth in size and treasure. They worried Sihar would no longer honor the friendly arrangements for water that quenched their fields and circulated their markets.

"He might impose a tax or another kind of ransom," King Ekam worried.

"And why not?" King Dve retorted. "He is powerful and strong enough to do so!"

"We are too vulnerable," King Treeni sighed, shaking his magnificent beard.

But the Three Kings had not the strength to defend or to invade. Even together, they barely matched Vishaka in soldiers or riches. It was better to have someone else risk the venture, they agreed, someone who had nothing to lose and everything to gain.

So Norom became their hope. Once installed, the Three Kings felt assured, Norom would guarantee them easy access to the water. After all, they reasoned, if they could put him on the Amber Throne, they could very well take him off it, too!

And, if Norom failed, they would still have good relations with King Sihar. No one would know of this secret pact. They could say Norom's troops came from runaways, his supplies stolen, and his audacity a curse from the gods. With this plan, the Three Kings toasted one another, they cannot lose!

Urma, too, thinks she cannot lose. Next day, she sends word to the Three Kings through her spies. *You can rely on us*, she writes on a sisal scroll, *should Norom fail*.

On the Trail

Sihar and his troops make camp a few days' ride from Norom's hideout. Sihar knows where it is for he could see bright, green bushes, larger and healthier than the rest, pointing the way. *Shenya's seeds*, he smiles to himself.

Sihar knows he can easily defeat Norom. Sihar has the best of his army in tow, whereas Norom scrabbles by with a band of bandits. But Sihar refrains from storming the hideout. Always cautious in war, he is even more so with Shenya in mind. He cannot risk injury to her in the confusion of battle. Sihar calls his most trusted general to his tent.

"Yes, my lord?" Amur salutes with a bow.

"I need you to spy for me, my friend."

"Of course, Sire."

"But, first, you must shave your head and put on a pilgrim's robe. Can you do that, Amur?"

The loyal subordinate hesitates not a moment. "Yes, Sire!"

"Good." Sihar pats him on the back. "You start tomorrow."

At dawn, Amur sets off in his new guise as a religious pilgrim. He sheds his soldier's leather straps for a robe of simple cotton cloth and straw sandals. Instead of the sharp-edged saber, shaped like a moon in half-glow, he carries the mendicant's bowl and a walking stick of scented *thakum* wood, found only in temples. His shorn head and face renounce all vanity to the world.

Amur walks for six days and six nights before reaching Norom's camp. By then, he truly resembles a mendicant: unkempt, unwashed, and unfed. Still, he cannot disguise his soldier's bearing and physique. He can feel Norom's men eyeing him with suspicion.

"I come to the pilgrimage only recently," he explains. "Having experienced too much war, I want nothing more of it."

Norom's men murmur in understanding. They often feel the same themselves.

The mendicant is welcomed into the camp. In their newfound goodwill, Norom's men share their meals with him. The mendicant cannot thank his hosts enough. He agrees heartily: they live in paradise!

For his part, Amur regales the camp with stories from his travels. (He borrows generously from the "Evening of Dreams.") The men cannot believe his fantastic tales, nor can they resist them. The mendicant is an unexpected and pleasant distraction, Norom's men agree. He thoroughly earns his keep!

They confide in him, in turn. Their good fortune, Norom's men whisper to the pilgrim, comes from their master's new hostage, a high Priestess.

"A high Priestess?!" Amur echoes in amazement. Kidnapping a Priestess in this part of the world incurs a heavy penalty. But curiosity overcomes all. "Where is she?" he asks, seemingly all innocence, craning his neck to catch sight of the prisoner.

"With him!" the men roar. They point to the cave that houses the hostage and from which their lord and master has yet to emerge. Amur is caught off-guard. *The Priestess with the tyrant?* Without thinking, Amur lets out a presumptuous query:

"Are they . . . ?"

Ghannaht, Norom's lieutenant, instantly jumps up, drawing his saber with eyes blazed into slits. The others follow suit, encircling Amur with the threat of death.

"Why so many questions, *Pilgrim*?!"

Amur quickly re-assumes the mendicant's humble pose.

"Apologies, fellow travelers," He bows hurriedly. "I have been too long removed from such earthly pleasures."

Norom's men stay their sabers menacingly. Then, just as quickly, they burst into ribald cheer, slapping the pilgrim on the back. The poor, deprived soul!

Amur the mendicant bids farewell early next morn.

"I must be on my way," he thanks his hosts, "to find my temple."

They wave him good-bye. Norom's hard-bitten men would never admit it but they will miss this pilgrim.

In due time, Amur the general returns to his own camp. He immediately reports to King Sihar in his tent.

"Norom has about two hundred men, all ruffians and the last of his army. His camp seems well protected. The men appear healthy and strong. Even their horses and dogs are in excellent condition. But we can overtake them easily. We have three times their number."

Sihar takes in the news. He is sitting behind a makeshift table with a map of the local terrain on it. Small, round stones sit on each corner of the scroll to keep it from flying with the restless wind. Trying to sound as usual, Sihar asks: "And . . . the Priestess?"

"I . . . did not see her, Sire, but she was at the camp."

Sihar detects the hesitance in his usually forthright general.

"Explain!" Sihar commands.

Amur pauses. Everyone knows of the King's high regard for the Priestess. Why are they here, after all? Amur does not relish telling him what could be either a profound betrayal on Shenya's part or a profound violation on Norom's. Still, it has to be done. Sihar, the King and the man, deserves no less. Amur steels himself.

"Norom the Tyrant has taken her into his abode, Your Majesty."

Sihar's heart stops, his mouth dries. He picks up a gourd of water to drink. It spills slightly.

"I see . . ." Sihar wipes his lip with the back of his left hand. It slides unconsciously to his pendant, now empty of the life-saving *mantra*.

Amur fails to mention that Norom and Shenya live in the cooking and storage cave, not the deposed King's own tent. To Amur, a lifelong soldier, the distinction is trivial.

But, had Sihar known, he would have detected straight away that not all is what it seems.

"Your orders, Sire?" The general breaks the awkward silence.

Sihar resumes a clear, calm voice. "Rest now, my friend. You have done well. We will plan in the morrow."

The general bows again then exits the tent. His guard informs him next day that His Majesty's lamp burned late into night, darkening only before the dawn.

Revival

Norom opens his eyes. *Where am I?* He struggles to speak but neither his body nor his mind will pay heed. Everything moves slowly, as if wading through a torrent of mud. Nothing seems familiar. He is sleeping in his usual silk comforts but on a bed of leaves . . . in a cave! A woman – *Who is she?* – is stirring something in a large, black pot . . . Heavily, brokenly, Norom's mind crawls back into wakefulness, triggering small movements in his arms and legs.

The woman looks up from her labors.

"Are you awake, Sire?"

That voice, Norom's mind elbows him. *Do you remember . . . ?*

"Priestess," Norom's voice croaks from disuse.

"Have some soup, Sire." Shenya drops by his side with a bowl of steaming sustenance. Norom gulps it down greedily. "How do you feel?" she asks with concern.

"Like an elephant danced on me," Norom groans. Shenya laughs, as much from relief as the silliness of it. Norom, too, feels reassured by her levity. "How long have I been away?"

"Six days and five nights, Sire."

"Ah . . . !" Norom slumps back at the news. The kidnapping, the return of his Throne – everything! – all jeopardized, once again, by this childhood affliction.

"You've had many such episodes, Sire?" Shenya probes lightly, delicately.

"Too many," Norom admits. He guesses that Shenya knows all about it. He guesses also, since they are both alive, his men do not. Without knowing why, Norom starts telling Shenya about his childhood.

⋆　⋆　⋆

His father and mother would hide him in a hole in the ground, with only an elderly nurse in attendance, whenever his affliction erupted. He was allowed to "return" only when the tremblings and foamings ended and he could resume normal speech. Norom's father, the King, could not permit others to know of his only son's possession by the spirits. They would have demanded his death! Yet everyone suspected. And their suspicions grew with the secrecy.

When older, Norom had a tunnel dug under his palace. It would shield the royal family from the elements, he explained, when traveling from one palace to the next. Yet only he had the key. Whenever he sensed a coming disturbance in mind or body, he hid in the tunnel, emerging only when the torment passed.

Soon, all forgot about the tunnel. But many wondered why Norom, now King, often disappeared for days with no apparent account.

To squash rumors of weakness or any kind of debility, Norom exerted his sovereign power against offenses real and imagined, major and trivial. He *had* to become a tyrant. Norom's subjects submitted to him because he was their King, but they never gave him the love or friendship he craved. His tyranny did not allow him to receive any, even when offered, for he feared intimacy would expose his secret, this unending, festering sore. And he became a tyrant even more from anger and loneliness.

★ ★ ★

"I envied Sihar and his Kingdom," Norom confesses. "I thought, if I had Vishaka, then I could be loved, too."

Shenya listens as no one has before in Norom's life. She knows his soul needs to heal. And her usual counsel, based on the wisdom of trees, will not do. He'd think she is making light of him. Shenya decides to speak from the heart.

"Be who you are, Sire, and your burden will lessen. My herbs can help you calm the fires that rage within your body. But you alone must calm the fires that rage within your heart."

Norom stares at his feet, dangling over the bed of leaves.

"Is it not too late for me, Priestess?" he asks, almost in a whisper.

"It is never too late, Sire, to be true to oneself."

The tyrant, her warden, turns to Shenya searchingly. *What are his eyes saying?* she asks herself.

Just then, Tandra enters the cave with a basketful of picks from the mountainside.

"Sire!" Tandra exclaims, overjoyed to see his master alive and well.

Norom does not recognize his former underling. Where Tandra had always bowed and scraped in his presence, with a matt of hair covering half his face, the cook now stands with a straight spine and square shoulders. He seems healthier and stronger. Definitely happier. For the first time in ten years, since his parents sold nine-year-old Tandra into royal servitude, Norom sees his attendant. He is of scrawny build but has a surprisingly pleasing face, with a square jaw, straight – even pert – nose, and sparkling eyes no longer downcast. Tandra falls on his knees by Norom, still lying like a newborn babe on the bed of leaves.

"How may thy servant aid thee?"

"Help us get up, Underling," Norom commands gruffly, returning to royal habit.

Unexpectedly and uncontrollably, Tandra recoils.

"His name is Tandra, Sire," Shenya prods gently, as if reminding Norom.

The former tyrant looks at the Priestess and the cook, knowing both had saved his life.

"Of course," Norom replies. "Tandra."

A crooked smile lights up the cook's face as he helps Norom rise from the bed of leaves.

The Rescue

Sihar is ready to make his move. Having scouted Norom's camp, he knows exactly how to proceed. He will strike at pre-dawn when the enemy is deeply asleep. The first wave of men will creep in, with daggers between their teeth and, on their backs, sacks of spider weave, the strongest netting on earth for tying prey. Their goal: to capture as many men, dogs, and horses on the ground as possible. Wound but do not kill, Sihar orders. These men are seasoned warriors, the King explains to his generals. They can be of service to Vishaka some day. They are with Norom not from loyalty or conviction but because they have nowhere else to go. Once they are given a choice

– especially an excellent one like Vishaka – they will abandon Norom without a second thought. The generals agree.

A second wave of men, Sihar continues, will secure the horses, the supplies, and the weaponry. Any man who tries to escape will be hobbled with swinging lassoes tied with river pebbles at the ends.

"We will bring up the rear," the King concludes, "with horses, spears, and arrows –"

Before Sihar can finish, a messenger crashes inside the tent, panting heavily.

"Sire!" The man kneels before his King. *A missive from Court?* Sihar expects the courier to hand him a rolled-up sisal scroll as usual. Instead, the courier points outside the tent. "They are here, Sire!"

"Who?"

Even the generals blink blankly.

"Norom the Tyrant and Shenya the Priestess!"

Sihar strides quickly to the surveillance platform. Using a bamboo shaft as telescope, he sees a regiment of roughly two hundred men, some on horses, others leading dogs, still a distance away but marching evenly toward their camp. Heading this band of bandits are two riders: Norom and Shenya.

Seeing Shenya at Norom's side, Sihar senses instinctively the tyrant could not have violated her. Yet Sihar's heart could not lift. This could only mean . . . The King clenches his jaw and chides himself inwardly. *Preoccupied with schoolboy hurts at a time like this!* Sihar orders his men to their stations with weapons primed and aimed. They are fortified and ready. *Were I so! How could she . . . ?* Sihar forces himself back to the scene at hand. Norom's men seem too open to engage in battle. Still, one never knows. *Indeed, one never knows . . .*

Sihar is camped at the top of a hill. By the time Norom's troops reach the bottom, a messenger hails with a white, triangular flag. *Surrender*, it signals.

"Admit the tyrant and the Priestess," Sihar orders. "Leave the rest in place."

Amur leads two guards down to meet Norom and his men. While conveying terms to the deposed King, Amur is surprised, then amused, to see Norom's men, especially Ghannaht, grinning broadly at him. *So they knew all along!*

Amur escorts Norom and Shenya up the hill while the rest of the men wait below. Sihar prepares to meet his rival and the woman for whom both men had risked going to war.

Norom and Shenya dismount when they see King Sihar approaching. Norom speaks first, folding his hands before him: "Greetings, O King."

Sihar, in turn, touches his forehead briefly. A courteous gesture, it is, nonetheless, decidedly less formal and less respectful than Norom's.

"Brother Norom," Sihar greets him dryly. He sees Shenya, smiling at him, a goatskin coat wrapped around her shoulders, her hair long and flowing in the wind. *More beautiful than ever!* Anger and jealousy suddenly flame up like errant embers caught afire. Sihar turns away, furrowing his brows. *Not the time or the place.*

Shenya's smile fades with bewilderment. *What's wrong?*

"Are you here to beg for mercy?" Sihar demands of Norom.

The response is startling.

"Yes, Sire."

Norom calls him "Sire." *Does this mean he recognizes us as his lord?* Sihar wonders. *How could events turn around so?* He must learn more.

"Come." Sihar extends an arm to Norom, as one sovereign to another. "Let us talk."

The News

News reaches Greybeard next evening. King Sihar is coming home at last! And with the former tyrant, Norom, as an ally, not an enemy captive! Everyone rejoices and celebrates. Vishakans light the path to the Royal Palace with torches and strew it with marigolds.

Everyone, that is, except Urma and Mandu. They cannot believe their ears. Norom an ally! This is the one move they had not anticipated.

Mandu sinks into stunned silence. Urma is just the opposite. She cannot stay still. Pacing back and forth, her heart pounds while her thoughts scatter like frightened crows. *What to do? What to do?* Now their secret will be out! Sihar will learn of their plot to kidnap Shenya, throwing the Court into disarray for three moons. What can they expect but the worst?

"We must notify the Three Kings, Father," Urma urges.

Mandu's eyes are glazed with defeat.

"And do what, my child?"

"To ally with us, of course! Norom will surely tell Sihar about the secret war against Vishaka, now that they are friends."

"Why would Sihar believe Norom?" Mandu wipes his brow. "He would say anything to save his hide now!"

"Sihar has eyes. He can see that Norom has ample supplies even in exile. Where do these come from? Especially for a deposed King?"

"And what do you propose we tell the Three Kings?" Mandu retorts testily.

Urma replies stonily: "That you and I will take Norom's place and lead the invasion from within."

"Invasion? From within? Against King Sihar?" Mandu heaves heavily. "The people *and* the army love him!"

"We must change that, then!"

"What could we *possibly* say that would turn the people against him?!"

A quiet calm descends upon Urma. She always likes a challenge. And this one is equal to all the typhoons in season. Her complexion, usually smooth and opaque, now turns translucent like plain coconut water. She sits down and speaks quietly, deliberately. "We will spread the rumor that Priestess Shenya has bewitched the King. Why else would he risk Throne and Kingdom to save her?"

Mandu shrinks with fear and conspiracy. "Would he not do the same for any valued advisor?"

"Yes but why attend to matters in person? A trusted general would have done just as well."

Mandu puts a fatherly hand on his daughter's shoulder. "What if, my child, he loves her?"

"King Sihar knows he cannot admit to such!" Urma shrugs off his arm impatiently, cheeks aflame. She walks to an open window and looks out as she speaks: "He would forfeit his Throne. We all know that, since time immemorial, it is forbidden by law for royalty to have private relations with any member of the Temple of Knowledge." Urma begins to smile and her eyes take on a distant stare. "To worsen our case against the Priestess, we will stir suspicion that she has taken up with Norom. She is a vixen who bewitches all men! We will demand that King Sihar put her to death for such treason! This will also lessen the power of the Temple of Knowledge. Once its reputation is besmirched, the Temple can no longer remain apart from our command." Urma starts to pace again, this time with purpose in every step. She continues: "To give us force, we will need soldiers from the Three Kings. They will arrest the King's Court. We will say that Greybeard and the others are also under Shenya's spell! The Three Kings' soldiers will hold off Sihar's men. The best are with him now. It would not be hard to convince those who remain. Besides, Sihar's soldiers will be wary, too. They are loyal to him but not his sorceress. We will say we are doing this for the good of King and Kingdom!"

Mandu begins breathing hard. A tidal wave seems to have swallowed him.

"My child," he beseeches his eldest and brightest, "let us admit defeat and take the consequences as they come. I am too old for this."

"I am not, Father!" Urma trembles with defiance and will. Just like a man to abandon a woman at the first sign of struggle! *No*, Urma vows, *I will not be like my father – nor will I be like my mother.* "I will fight alone if I have to, Father," Urma states, her voice strangely flat.

Mandu knows he cannot stop her.

"Alright, child," he concedes. "What is your will?"

Urma summons her best spy to deliver this message to the Three Kings: *Norom exposed. Send troops. I will command.* She signs it, *Mandu*.

The Three Kings promptly respond. Next morn, their soldiers march stolidly toward Vishaka.

En Route

At camp, Norom reveals all to Sihar: the plot to kidnap Shenya, Mandu and Urma, the Three Kings.

Sihar listens quietly. It pains him to know of such treachery from those he considers close friends and allies.

It pains him even more that the man enlightening him has also captured the Priestess, body and soul.

"Why are you so willing to betray your conspirators and befriend us?" Sihar presses Norom.

The deposed King speaks after a long pause: "A Throne on its own is no more than a place to sit. It is the love of a people that makes a King. Even if I could conquer Vishaka, I could never rule it."

"Such wisdom, brother, where comes it?" Sihar tests Norom further, not quite believing his former enemy.

"A Priestess," Norom answers simply.

"Ah!" Sihar leans back on his pillows. He understands all too well.

Norom gives Sihar a sideways glance. From his reaction, Norom detects more at stake between King and Priestess than just sovereign and advisor. He sighs inwardly, wishing his new friends well.

A Late-Night Visit

That evening, after dining with Norom, Sihar calls on Shenya in her tent. *Three moons of hard riding and tracking to find her*, he chides himself, *and yet how my knees tremble!*

The King addresses the Priestess stiffly: "We trust you are well . . . have all the comforts?"

Not expecting a visit from His Majesty at this time of night, Shenya quickly rises from her mat and bows with folded hands. She has on a simple evening robe, belted loosely at the waist. Sihar cannot overlook the robe's enchanting embrace of Shenya's body. Her hair is still down, full and flowing, though a comb has seen it of late. A thick, fat candle of jasmine and beeswax glows nearby. It casts a rosy hue on Shenya's cheeks amidst cleverly dancing shadows, inviting a . . . *Stop it!*, he commands himself.

"Yes," she answers quickly (*nervously?*) while clutching the fold of her robe in front, making sure nothing is revealed. Sihar continues inspecting Shenya's tent, as if on duty. Shenya senses his discomfort. *Why does he seem a stranger? Have these three moons changed that much between us?*

"Our brother lord, Norom . . ." Sihar speaks abruptly.

"Yes, Sire?"

"You now know him well . . . by now?"

"I suppose so, Sire . . ."

"What kind of man is he?" Sihar asks tersely. "Can we trust him?"

"I believe so," Shenya answers slowly and sincerely. "He's caused his share of trouble, Sire, but, deep down, he is a good man."

"Would you trust him with your life?" Sihar returns, seemingly casual in his query.

Shenya smiles. *What kind of question is that?*

"Haven't I already, Sire?"

Somehow her answer displeases Sihar. A frown flits across his face then, just as quickly, it disappears.

Sihar looks every inch the sovereign as he stands there, with both hands folded behind his back. The King and the Priestess face each other awkwardly, silently. Finally, Sihar holds out one hand and turns it over. In the center of his palm are two tiny strands of pearls.

"We believe these belong to you, Priestess. Finding them helped us greatly in finding you."

She cries out with delight. "Majesty! I feared never to see them again –"

"Yes," Sihar cuts her short. "They were most useful." He hands them to her then leaves.

Sihar's Dream

Back in his own tent, Sihar admits he cannot blame Norom for falling in love with Shenya. After all, hadn't he himself . . . ? But Sihar cannot grant equal magnanimity to Shenya. She gave herself to Norom, so easily and so quickly – three moons! – when *they* have known each other for . . . No, no! Sihar shoves aside these regrets. War is averted and all can return to as it was . . . Or can it? By this time, the King's weary body pulls him deeply into slumber. And he rests like he had not since before Shenya disappeared.

Soon, he enters into a dream:

They are sitting under the shade of the Ancient One, by the bubbling brook. Shenya is next to him. Her hair is down, long and silky, gliding over bare shoulders. She is not in her priestly robes but a commoner's dress. It has a simple blue-and-white pattern, like Tang porcelain. A red hibiscus, tucked in the middle of the bodice, livens the colors. The top consists of one strip of cloth, tied with a knot in the back, leaving the midriff open. Below is a sarong *that falls just above her ankles and folded over naked legs and feet.*

Before them is a large palm leaf. On it is placed several smoked fish beside a small mound of fragrant, white rice. Next to the palm leaf is a teak platter filled with brown longans, still on their vines, and three round, fuzzy, blushing peaches. In the distance, Sihar can see huge white lilies, large as elephants. Each petal undulates gently into a pointed tip, as if designed to catch a dewdrop only to let it spill carelessly, nonchalantly onto the next petal. A deep red centers each flower, heavy with pollen. "See, Sire –" Shenya holds out her arms with a big, bright smile, as if to hug this beautiful, wonderful world. "What riches surround us! We are blessed."

Sihar wakes with a start. *A most unusual though pleasant dream . . . What does it mean?*

Before he can contemplate further, an attendant rushes into Sihar's tent.

"Sire!" he alerts the King. "Minister Mandu has led an army to greet us – or to fight us!"

The Request

It is a clear, brilliant day. Sea blue froths from above. Yellow wildflowers wave from below.

Two armies face each other on an open, grassy field. Mountains sit behind one; a forest frames the other. Colorful banners on both sides flap briskly in the breeze.

Sihar's men number eight hundred, with Norom's counted in for good measure. Mandu heads a regiment of two thousand. Half comes from Sihar's regular army; the rest, the Three Kings. Sihar can tell who is where from the banners: the first four rows carry Vishaka's green-and-white, followed by the orange-and-purple flags of King Ekam, the gold-and-silver ones of King Dve, and the blue-and-yellow banners of King Treeni. Sihar senses another plot brewing, given what he now knows about Mandu and Urma and the Three Kings. But he cannot reveal his move just yet. He needs to survey the lay of the land first.

Riding Duan, Sihar leads his men in front and stops short of Mandu's army. By military standards of the day, the length of ten elephants, if lined from trunk to tail, distances the two armies. With Amur beside him, Sihar trots up to the halfway mark to meet Mandu. The Minister of Grains does the same with Sihar's second highest-in-command, Kalan, next to him. The four men are now abreast of one another. They can speak without shouting.

"Thank you for welcoming us home," Sihar addresses Mandu and Kalan, not without a touch of irony. "But you needn't have brought so many friends with you."

"Alas, Sire –" the Minister of Grains bows unctuously from his saddle "– I am burdened with an unusual but also an undeniable request from your men."

"Oh?" Sihar tries to sound calm.

"They believe the Priestess has bewitched Your Majesty and ask for her execution." Mandu lowers his eyes, pretending to shield his embarrassment but, really, to mask his duplicity.

Sihar turns to Kalan. "Is this true?"

His general bows in response. "Yes, Sire."

"What is the basis for this?!" Sihar demands, now fully incensed.

Mandu answers with his usual ministerial polish, although, to Sihar's expert ear, it rattles a little.

"Your Majesty abandoned Throne and Kingdom, leaving both vulnerable to the ambitions of others, to rescue a mere Priestess, were it not for our friends, the Three Kings."

Before Sihar can respond, Kalan raises his right hand, angled sharply at the elbow, and rounds it into a fist. At this signal, all one thousand of Sihar's men dismount and kneel on the field, their swords held high above their heads with both hands.

"Your men," Mandu continues, now more brazenly, "refuse to go on until you agree to their request."

"We are loyal to you, Sire, but not the Priestess," Kalan adds.

Sihar considers the situation. He cannot expose Mandu's plot with the Three Kings. His men would think it a distraction. Neither can he dismiss his men's request, for that would incite a rebellion.

The King turns to his Minister: "What do you want?"

A smile creeps into Mandu's voice.

"Allow us to escort Your Majesty back to Vishaka. Once at Court, we will hold a public trial of the Priestess before executing her. We will conduct all the proper rites and rituals so no one can curse us for violating a Priestess." He stops to catch his breath, then continues: "Meanwhile, Your Majesty will return to the Palace. All royal protocol and dignity will be accorded but Your Majesty cannot come and go as you please. We will need to conduct rites and rituals on you too, Sire, to purge you of her witchcraft."

Sihar's eyes meet Amur's. The two men, friends since childhood, understand they must submit – for now. Sihar nods to Kalan. The second-in-command raises his fist again and Sihar's men, seeing that their King has agreed to their request, rise in one movement and swing their swords high in affirmation, thundering a collective "Ho!"

Mandu swells with triumph. Never could he imagine such power! Still, a nagging unease tugs at him. He expected the besotted King to defend the Priestess to the end, provoking a battle of unequals that would ultimately close this charade. Now they must play it out at Court. *Never mind*, Mandu assures himself. *We still have him*.

Mandu and Kalan escort Sihar and Amur back to their side of the field. Upon reaching, Kalan calls out: "Arrest the Priestess!"

Instead, Sihar's men reach for their weapons. *Why is the order coming from Kalan and not Amur or His Majesty? Have they not just spent three moons of hard riding to* rescue *the Priestess?* Sihar motions to his men to stand down. He signals to Amur.

The King's trusted friend and general rides up to Shenya and bows formally. The general extends an invitation as if to a tea party: "Priestess Shenya, would you be so kind as to follow me?"

Shenya cannot decipher what is happening. Like everyone at her end of the field, she is bewildered to see Sihar's men, suddenly dismounting and surrendering their weapons, only to rise again and swing them in celebration. *What does this mean?* Perplexed yet not wishing to disturb, she follows Amur obediently on her horse.

Norom and Tandra exchange worried looks as she passes by.

The King's Return

Back at Court, Urma arranges a lavish banquet for the evening of the King's return. She invites all of Vishaka's best families, even those arrested for "succumbing to the spell." Urma adds three special guests: Kings Ekam, Dve, and Treeni. To them, Urma wants to display her largesse: *See how in command we are!* To the rest of the Court, she displays her power: *Do not cross us, for we have the Three Kings!*

Urma hurries to greet Sihar in his outer chamber. Attendants rush to and fro with muslin towels and jugs of water, freshened with jasmine and lime, to welcome the tired King. Sihar is in the midst of taking off his sword and straps when Urma arrives.

"Sire." She curtsies deeply. "I could say the Kingdom and the people are ecstatic to have you back. But I can't." She cocks her head coyly at his raised brow. "For no one could be more ecstatic than I." As she rises gracefully,

Urma makes sure her long veil, a translucent strip of apricot silk chiffon sprinkled with glittering stars, falls ever so seductively over her bare, brown shoulders. Her hair, fashioned high above in a twist pinned by an orchid flower the color of the sea at dusk, clears her long, slender neck, perfect for a kiss. Sihar notices her special allure that afternoon.

"You are too gracious, as always, Lady Urma," he replies.

"We have prepared a special banquet to welcome you home, Majesty. I attended to all the details myself. I hope it will please you, Sire."

"We are sure 'twill be so, Lady Urma. You have done too much."

"Nothing is too much for you, Sire." Urma gazes up at Sihar. *This is going well!* she self-congratulates. *He seems more open to me than before. Perhaps time away from the Priestess has dampened his ardor for her.* Urma can't help but let slip a little smile.

Sihar pauses, and looks down at her meaningfully.

"You should smile more often, Urma." The King's intimate tone is unusual, unexpected. Urma's satiny skin glows even more. Before she can reply, Sihar speaks again. "We know of the special circumstances of our return," he smiles ruefully, "but could we trouble you to add one more guest for tonight?"

"Of course, Sire! Who, may I ask?"

"Our brother lord, Norom."

"Norom the Tyrant . . . ?" Urma's cheeks now flush redly.

"Yes," Sihar replies. "He is, of late, Vishaka's friend. He recognizes our suzerainty over his Kingdom and should be treated as an honored guest."

"Of – of course, Sire." Urma curtsies again, this time to avoid Sihar's eyes.

He approaches her and places his hands on her shoulders.

"We know of your deeds, Urma."

"Sire . . . ?"

"We know you conspired with Norom to kidnap the Priestess."

Urma lowers her eyes. She answers a little too quickly, breathlessly. "It was to save you, Sire . . . and – and the Kingdom. She put a spell on you!"

"We appreciate your concern," Sihar counters evenly. "But you should have come to us first, rather than complain to others." Urma tries to explain. But Sihar cuts her off. "Let us speak of it no more," he commands wearily. "Leave us. We need to rest."

"Yes, Sire." Urma curtsies again to leave. This time, she cares not where her veil falls.

The Banquet

The banquet that evening is a glittering, glorious affair, held on King Sihar's favorite terrace by the lotus pond. Tiny candles flicker everywhere, even on the lily pads. Garlands of purple freesia, twined with red bougainvillea, drape the halls, the pillars, the steps, the divans, and the kitchens, mixing the mouth-watering aroma of the evening's menu with the heart-stealing perfume of the flowers. Large, flat cushions – some square, some round – ensure comfortable sitting. They are placed one next to the other in two curved rows that face each other, forming a semi-circle. Raw silk in Vishaka's royal green-and-white covers every cushion. Special incense smokes the area with fragrant mystery. It also discourages visits by lizards, ants, flies, and other interlopers. Court musicians grace the ear with melodies of lightness and dreams and fairies dancing with gossamer wings. A balmy, star-studded sky sparkles benevolently from above.

Shenya looks up at the same sky through the bars over her head and prays. *O Merciful Universe, help sustain me through this time of tribulation . . .* She is held in a prison underground. It is a hole dug deep enough to need a ladder to reach the top but barely large enough to sleep without folding her legs. Just then, Tandra's head appears, blotting out the stars.

"Priestess!" he calls down with cupped hands. "Are you alright?"

Shenya gladdens to this friendly face but she could not risk having him thrown into prison.

"Yes!" she whispers back quickly. "I am fine. Please don't worry!"

"I brought you some sustenance, Priestess." Tandra pushes through the bars a bundle wrapped in coarse cotton and a gourd of water. She catches both gratefully.

"Now go!" she insists, and he does.

Shenya unfolds the bundle. In it are two smaller packages, one sealed in palm leaf; the other, a thin sheet of rush matting. Shenya opens the palm leaf first and smiles. It contains two pieces of charred flatbread. Tandra knows that is her most favored treat. Unrolling the rush matting, Shenya's eyes widen with wonder. Before her are her priestly robes. They are freshly laundered and precisely folded. Lying on top are two strands of small pearls, the ones she uses to tie up her hair.

Something's afoot, she suspects.

A Glittering Affair

King Sihar sits cross-legged on the main dais, raised slightly on a platform above the others. Before him is a large brass plate on which are placed small dishes of various delicacies. Three kinds of curry – red, green, and black – invite him to dip thin, flour pancakes; an array of lettuce leaves, yellow sprouts, and slivers of green onion, topped with cuts of lime, accompany *satayed* prawns, dripping with thick, spicy sauce; a bamboo ladle filled with whitefish steamed in ginger and sprinkled with sprigs of coriander, almond bits, and pineapple juice await tasting; likewise with a plate of scallops mashed with anchovies and yam; wild boar in a small clay pot simmered for hours in wine and papaya and pine nuts; two different soups, one with lotus root floating in hot, clear chicken broth and the other, cold, crushed black sesame in creamy coconut yogurt flecked with pomegranate seeds. Various pickled vegetables sit to one side, each balancing the five tastes of sweet, sour, salty, spicy, and bitter. These are paired with steaming saffron rice, loosely oiled with cashews, on a palm leaf; and, of course, various fruits and sweets.

Radee wine flows plentifully from invisible servers with invisible hands.

Orchid blossoms garnish each dish, whether it is served on teak platters or Tang porcelain or the traditional palm leaf. A different vinegar drink, brimming from carved walnut shells, cleanses the palate between each course. Made from collected dewdrops and fermented fruit, it stimulates even as it refreshes.

Seated below King Sihar, to his left is Norom; to his right, the Three Kings. Each presides over a similar spread of delights. On their left and right, respectively, are arrayed the rest of Vishaka's nobility, including Greybeard. With King Sihar at the center, the gathering engages in wit and worldliness while enjoying the evening's many entertainments.

First comes an ode to the King. The song praises Sihar's great virtues and victories, his grasp of the present and foresight for the future as well as respect for the past, and, of course, his noble, heroic lineage that honors the people with its love.

Everyone sways along as they savor every bite of every morsel of every dish.

Urma is most pleased. Everything is going so well! All the frenzy and planning of the past few days have not been for naught.

The singing ends to enthusiastic applause. As the musicians collect their instruments to make way for the next performance, a dance by Vishaka's children (more adult fare to follow), an unexpected commotion erupts. It comes from the corner of honored guests.

King Ekam is choking, food flying in all directions. A rotund man, he knocks over the dishes by his side, seemingly in a fight . . . with himself! He causes such a stir that the music stops, the chatter ends, and all turn toward him with concern.

"See to him!" Urma commands an attendant.

But, before anyone can reach him, King Ekam stops choking and stands up, his face red and his body shaking like a leaf in monsoon. He declares loudly for all to hear: "Minister Mandu and his daughter, Lady Urma, plotted with King Norom to take over the Amber Throne!"

Gasps hush the gathering. Urma and Mandu seem struck by lightning, so petrified and ashen are they.

Now King Dve stands up! With the same red face and trembling form, a more disturbing sight due to his extreme thinness, he reveals: "When King Norom surrendered to King Sihar, Minister Mandu asked us for soldiers to arrest the Court and its King!"

Disbelief floods the gathering, daunting even the crickets.

King Treeni, a bejeweled man with a magnificent, manicured beard, also rises from his seat. Reddened and quaking like the others, King Treeni delivers the final exposé. He points a quivering, gem-encrusted finger at Urma and bellows forth: "It was Lady Urma who spread the rumor that Priestess Shenya had put a spell on King Sihar!"

Urma's eyes whiten with anger and fear but she remains outwardly calm.

"Clearly," Urma defends herself, a vision in haughty azure, "the Priestess has also bewitched our friends, the Three Kings!"

"Their Majesties are telling the truth!" Norom jumps up. "Lady Urma and her father, Minister Mandu, proposed that I kidnap Priestess Shenya to weaken King Sihar's resolve. The Three Kings supported this plot. They feared Vishaka's new growth in size and power, and worried about their access to water."

The Three Kings, now seated, redden further and exchange furtive looks.

"Why should we believe *you*, a deposed tyrant?" Urma challenges, the roots of her hair ablaze with indignation. "How do we know you are not in conspiracy with the Three Kings even now?"

Sihar has to admire Urma's fortitude, if not her daring.

"Because –" Greybeard rises from his seat "– we have evidence."

Murmurs rampage through the crowd. *Outrageous! Incredible! What's next?*

Greybeard steps to the center of the gathering and draws from within his sleeve three sisal scrolls. "These –" he waves them high in the air "– are the messages sent by Minister Mandu and Lady Urma to our neighbors, the Three Kings."

"How . . . ?" Mandu ventures weakly.

"We have our ways, Minister," Greybeard returns meaningfully to his brother minister.

Kalan instantly draws his sword at Mandu.

"And to think I almost battled my own sovereign for you!" The Minister of Grains cringes visibly.

"Calm, General." King Sihar interjects with a raised hand. "We have been in communication with our neighbors, the Three Kings, all along. We could not inform you so the plotters would reveal their hand."

Kalan sheathes his sword reluctantly, and the Three Kings nod solicitously toward King Sihar and each other.

Urma's eyes narrow. *So Greybeard knew all along, the deceptive old snake!* The Three Kings must have consorted with all sides, making her think they supported her, while divulging their designs to Greybeard – and from him to King Sihar. No wonder Sihar accepted Mandu's escort so easily!

"Why this elaborate ruse, Minister," Urma picks up where her father couldn't, "when such evidence was already at hand?"

"We had to unmask you before all," Greybeard answers, "and with your co-conspirators in attendance. No one could accuse us of maligning you with fabrications."

Color begins to drain from Urma's being. Even as he charges her with treason, the Minister of Rites, that consummate politician, bows gallantly to Lady Urma.

King Sihar proclaims: "Let one and all know, and for all time, that our neighbors have nothing to fear from Vishaka. We will always honor our water arrangements with them. For their lack will become Vishaka's, if we are not generous."

The Three Kings hearten to King Sihar's declaration. They thought devious diplomacy the only means of ensuring water from Vishaka. Never did they consider that Vishaka would suffer along with them should their Kingdoms parch through war or taxes. Now they realize that Sihar would never hurt them. Doing so would hurt Vishaka itself!

"We pay homage –" the Three Kings genuflect in unison "– to Your Majesty's brilliance."

Sihar continues: "What we cannot understand – or forgive – is why Minister Mandu and Lady Urma, prized members of our own Court, would so assail a personage as Priestess Shenya, who has done nothing but honor our Realm with her wise counsel?"

Mandu lowers his head in shame and defeat. Words utterly fail him. But Urma is not to be foiled. She has no more to lose.

"I may have spread the rumor, Sire, but was I wrong? Did not Priestess Shenya bewitch Your Majesty? Why else would my lord abandon Throne and Kingdom to rescue a mere Priestess?"

Sihar pauses. Everyone knows of The Law. It prohibits alliances of any kind between Throne and Temple. Members of the Temple could serve as advisors equally to all Kingdoms but no more than this. Before, too many generations had spilled blood and tears to capture the Temple's knowledge so one Kingdom could topple another. Yet the devastations of war erased any victories gained. Finally, the Ancestors agreed, the Temple would stand alone, subject to no single Kingdom's decrees yet open to all who needed its service. In exchange, members of the Temple could travel freely throughout all the lands, gathering knowledge wherever they may. To maintain trust and order in the Universe, all agreed that any and all violators from the Temple would be executed (they would be too dangerous, otherwise) and those in the royal house dethroned (without a Kingdom, they would be nothing).

With this history before them, Sihar cannot admit his feelings for Shenya. But neither can he repudiate her. Both would amount to the same, turning Urma's ugly rumor into truth.

Urma senses Sihar's hesitation. She can almost taste the sweet honey of success. *She has him!* Color surges through her body, down to each toe and fingertip. Only one thing more is needed to perfect her triumph.

"Bring the Priestess!" she orders. "Let her answer for her crimes."

The guards turn to their King for permission. Sihar nods and they leave immediately to fetch the prisoner. Sihar cannot object to Urma's demand. It would make him seem guilty or, worse, weak.

Before long, Shenya appears. The gathering gasps again, more so from admiration than surprise. Instead of her prisoner's rags, dirty and torn, Shenya arrives in her pristine, priestly robes. Luminous in the evening's thousand candles, she seems to float to the center of the gathering. Shenya's hair is neatly and elegantly wrapped atop her head with two thin strands of pearls. Like the rest gathered there, Sihar cannot take his eyes off her. She appears thinner and paler than when he saw her last, on the field with the yellow wildflowers and the two armies, but her spirit remains, as ever, strong, clear, and beautiful. He takes in a deep breath and forces himself to speak.

"Priestess Shenya," he addresses her formally. "Lady Urma claims you have bewitched the Throne, the Court, and now our guests, the Three Kings. What say you to this charge?"

"If that is the case," Shenya responds evenly, "how is it that I am the prisoner?"

Many in the audience nod in agreement. Others look confused.

Taking Shenya's lead, Sihar questions Urma: "Priestess Shenya has never met our neighbors, the Three Kings. How could she bewitch them?"

Urma does not expect this reversal. Instead of Shenya on trial, it is now she! Having the Priestess appear in person is a mistake, she realizes too late. Whenever Sihar and Shenya are together, they make too formidable a team.

Urma's heart pounds hard and fast. She can barely breathe. *Think, think!* she commands herself. She must alter her line without changing her charge. She scours the gathering. Everyone's face is a sea of blurs – except, when her eyes alight on the Three Kings, her mind recalls them choking and spitting out food before making their damning revelations.

"The food!" Urma bursts forth. "She must have affected the food!"

All put down their tantalizing morsels. *What else lurks within?!*

Sihar cannot refute this latest charge. He, too, wants to know what compelled the Three Kings to confess and so suddenly.

"Bring out the chefs!" he orders.

Several guards run to the kitchen, escorting out the five men responsible for the evening's banquet. They prostrate themselves before their King, too frightened to do anything else.

"Chefs," Sihar addresses them kindly, "please have no fear. You will not be punished for anything you say."

The five men's limbs loosen slightly but they still keep their heads close to the ground.

The Master Royal Chef finally speaks for the rest: "Sire, we have done nothing to the food other than to make it delicious." The chef's simple honesty releases a ripple of twitters among the gathering. Certainly, no one could dispute *that*!

"Liar!" Urma growls, her face a dark mask of outrage. "One of you is an accomplice! Who is it? If you don't come forth, I'll have you flogged!"

The five chefs tremble abjectly.

"Stop!" A voice calls out from the dark. A scrawny young man emerges from one corner of the terrace. Tandra walks up to King Sihar and bows.

"'Twas I who put special herbs in the food for the Three Kings," Tandra confesses. "But these herbs can only force out the truth. They cannot create what is not there."

"Underling, you serve Lord Norom, do you not?" Urma demands. She had seen Tandra attending to Norom after they arrived at Court.

"Yes," Tandra replies. "I serve my lord Norom. But I have a name. It is Tandra."

"Even so, *Underling*," Urma stresses his station with contempt, "why did you spice the Three Kings' food?" Urma's sharp intelligence does not fathom that this one strike of venom against someone she considers a worthless servant poisons, instead, the entire gathering against her.

"To help Priestess Shenya," Tandra answers forthrightly.

"See?" Urma crows in triumph. "This man, this *underling*, is also under her spell!"

"If I am under her spell, my lady," Tandra continues unperturbed, "it is because she gave me a name." Tandra then recounts to the gathering how Shenya is the first person in his life to recognize him, praise him, and confer upon him a name that, in fact, he had chosen himself. And Tandra describes how this made him feel, like he can stand straight and throw back his shoulders and *breathe*, in contrast to his previously crouched and cowed existence.

Eyes glisten and hearts soften. If the Priestess could cast a spell, the gathering avows, then it is a good one! It makes people speak the truth, realize their being, and spread happiness. In fact, others recall, the Priestess had given many a fine counsel to King Sihar, helping the Kingdom thrive and prosper. And what about the "Evening of Dreams"? The notion came from King Sihar but wasn't he aided by the Priestess to conceive of it? Wasn't she the one who gave him the principle of "the orchid and the tree"?

Urma can feel the gathering slanting towards *them* and away from her. She throws out a final attack.

"Sire, if I am guilty of treason, then it is only to preserve The Law. It prohibits an alliance, of *any* kind, between the Throne and the Temple. I was not alone in seeing how the Priestess was becoming close to Your Majesty. To keep the Universe in peace and harmony, it is the Throne's duty to repudiate the Priestess. Else others would suspect the Throne of a secret love for her!"

Sihar looks at Shenya, standing there, so alone and so beautiful. He also gives Norom a glance.

"How can we speak of love," the King parries, "when the Priestess feels for another?"

Shenya's eyes flash with anger and disappointment and hurt. *How could he . . . ?!*

Norom catches the exchange between Sihar and Shenya, and knows he has to help his friends. Only he can correct their mutual misjudgment. Yet he must do so without damage to either.

"The Priestess is pure in body and soul!" Norom declares.

"And I can bear witness!" adds Tandra.

At first, stunned silence grips the gathering. Then, suddenly, raucous laughter breaks through. Drama has turned into comedy. *Hilarious!* Shenya can contain her fury no longer.

"What matters love or this talk of feelings!" she exclaims bitterly. "I gladly submit to execution than endure such humiliation –"

"*NO!*" The cry thunders through the terrace. Several doves flap off in fright. A frog hops back into the pond for shelter.

All turn to Sihar whose voice still echoes in their ears. Uncontrollably and unwittingly, the King has revealed the man. That which is buried deep inside his heart, denied admission even to himself, is now exposed to all. It is true, after all. He loves the Priestess.

A dry heave half-catches Shenya in the chest, tripping her breath. Her one moment of impulsiveness has led to the King's irreparable indiscretion.

Urma wins, finally. But, oddly, she cannot enjoy the moment. Like all at the gathering, she, too, is bereft of words.

King Ekam finally steps forward and bows to King Sihar.

"The Law is the law, brother lord. Your Majesty must leave the Throne or the Priestess is executed. If not, we will lose order in the Universe."

Greybeard once again comes before the gathering.

"Let us consider a compromise," the Minister of Rites suggests. "The people of Vishaka love our King Sihar.

They would not take kindly to his sudden departure, even if demanded by The Law. Nor would they accept execution of the Priestess. She has gained much goodwill here."

"What do you propose, then, Minister?" asks King Dve.

"What would help to retain harmony in the Universe?" Greybeard returns. Allowing the Three Kings to decide, he knows, will prevent others from learning of Sihar's transgression.

"Let us confer –" King Treeni motions to his fellow sovereigns. Greybeard joins them.

Moments of eternity later, all four reappear. The Minister of Rites announces: "Our neighbors, in their eminent graciousness, have decided that King Sihar may remain on the Throne and the Priestess return to the Temple of Knowledge . . ." The terrace sighs with audible relief. ". . . on one condition."

Sihar and Shenya brace for the judgment.

"And that is . . . ?" Sihar prompts tensely.

King Ekam answers: "King Sihar will marry the Lady Urma!"

King Dve explains: "Only in this way can we ensure King Sihar's total severance from the Priestess."

King Treeni adds: "And only in this way can we ensure Vishaka's total unity from within!"

Greybeard raises his cup: "Let us be the first to congratulate King Sihar and Queen Urma!"

Everyone rises and toasts the new Royal Couple.

Long Live the King! Long Live the Queen! Long Live Vishaka!

The Temple of Knowledge

Shenya surveys her old chamber at the Temple. *Strange*, she thinks as her eyes fall on the simple room, a rush mat on a raised platform, next to the camphor chest that serves as her desk under an open window. *Everything is the same and yet so different*. She unfolds the bundle of cloth brought back from the Palace. Out tumble a few items: a change of clothing, a few seeds, and a locket of jade and ruby.

* * *

"Take it," Sihar had urged, pushing the pendant into her hands, the night before. "I want you to have it. Thank you for everything . . ."

Shenya quieted him with her hand on his lips.

"There's no need."

Their eyes met in mutual recognition. Words no longer sufficed.

It was a stolen moment. Ever since the night of the banquet, the Palace made sure to keep them apart. But Norom had arranged one last meeting so the King could bid farewell to his Priestess. Tandra stood watch outside while Sihar, at last, could hold in his arms the woman he had loved since their first meeting in the forest.

"Let me give you something, too," Shenya offered. She fumbled with the two strands of pearls around her hair until a mass of black glory cascaded down. She shoved the pearls toward Sihar. He kissed the hands that held them, now encased within his own.

"Urma will be my wife," Sihar vowed to Shenya, "but you are my heart and soul and spirit, now and forever."

Shenya could only smile through her tears.

* * *

Back at the Temple, Shenya returns to her usual duties. But try as she might, she cannot concentrate as before.

During the day, she has no appetite; at night, no sleep. One day, Shenya faints in the noonday heat while planting her seeds. She finds herself waking in the Temple's cool infirmary, a large gourd of water next to a Tang bowl on a small stand by her bed – and the finely lined face of the Abbess peering down at her. Concern melts into a smile when she sees Shenya stirring.

"That's better, dear one." The Abbess smoothes Shenya's brow with a wizened hand that feels, surprisingly, soft and supple. "You must wear a hat next time."

"Please forgive me, Learned One, for causing so much trouble."

"Trouble?" the Abbess bounces the word. "You are anything but, dear one. Though, I must say –" the Abbess pokes Shenya teasingly in the ribs "– your bones protrude more of late. Are you so used to Palace fare now?"

Instead of a laugh or a smile, as would be her wont, Shenya bursts into tears. The Abbess chastises herself for mentioning anything to do with Sihar. Still, she thinks, this might be a good time to bring out what has been hidden for too long. "Dear one, please do not make things harder on yourself than necessary. What happened has happened. It was *karma*."

"I cannot accept that, Learned One," Shenya cries even more. "Why was I given love, then have it taken away so abruptly, so absolutely, before it even had a chance to flower? Is the Universe so cruel?"

"Ah . . ."

"I never pursued a woman's usual comforts, like husband and children, for I had another calling, equally noble. But with Sihar, I thought, perchance, I was wrong?" Shenya cannot stop now even if she wants to. She covers her face in shame and despair.

The Abbess gently pries open Shenya's hands.

"Dear one, I have something to show you." The Abbess reaches inside her robe and extracts a fragment of silk, the color of faded pomegranates and threaded in gold. "This *mantra* was given to me by your fine King Sihar." Shenya looks up despite herself. "He gave it to me the day he came to appeal for your presence at the Palace. He thought he had lost all hope when suddenly he presented this to me in farewell. I recognized it right away for what it was and decided to persuade you to join him at Court."

Shenya cannot take her eyes from the silk fragment.

"What is it?"

"Can you read the *mantra*?" The Abbess points to the words sewn in gold thread. Shenya shakes her head. The threading has faded too much. The Abbess closes her eyes and recites:

> *When* karma *comes, it springs from a source eternal.*
> *When* karma *is spent, that is also a course most natural.*

The Abbess opens her eyes and withdraws from the same spot in her robe an almost identical strip of silk cloth, also the color of faded pomegranates and threaded in gold. She pieces them together into a perfect match. She continues to recite, this time with her eyes open, but staring into the distance:

> *With* karma *we must be at ease,*
> *For the sentiments of* karma *last long, indeed.*

"I don't understand, Learned One," Shenya admits to her Abbess.

"These two fragments of silk bear an old story," the Abbess starts slowly. She looks down to even out an imagined wrinkle in her robe. "It tells of two hearts which had beat as one but, due to life's infinite wisdom, they had to separate. Yet their love was precious enough to carry them through to the end." The Abbess takes in a deep breath before continuing.

"Like you, I once advised a sovereign. And, like you, I fell wholly and utterly in love with my King." The Abbess nods knowingly to Shenya, now wholly captivated. The Abbess goes on: "He was a man as noble inside as he was outside. Even though I was two cycles older,[1] we understood each other implicitly. We knew, of course, that The Law prohibited any private relations between us. Yet The Law could not dictate against love in the mind and in the soul.

"One day, my sovereign visited a neighboring Kingdom. His host was a great friend and ally. The friend's son, it was well known, drank and gambled and played with women to his detriment. At the welcoming banquet, the son imbibed too much as usual and had to be carried away by attendants. The son's consort was left forlorn at her table. My sovereign felt sorry for her but guessed that she'd had many a similar occasion. He gave it no second thought.

"That night, just when my sovereign blew out the first of three candles, to ready for sleep, the consort appeared in his chamber, disguised as a maid. She beseeched him to bed her. She needed to produce an heir for the royal house, she whispered feverishly in the half-dark, but her husband, the Prince, despised her, as their marriage was arranged without his consent, like much of his life under his imperious father. No one else would dare to help. He was her only hope.

"'How do you know we will succeed?' my sovereign asked. 'That I am the one?'

"'I dreamed of this union and the little boy who will come of it,' she explained. 'He will become a great and benevolent leader, bringing peace and prosperity to our Kingdom. But the dream also told me I must do this now or be forever doomed.' My sovereign looked at her incredulously. 'I am an interpreter of dreams,' she added.

"The woman was young and appealing, and my sovereign no monk. They did their deed and nine moons later a son was born.

"My sovereign confessed to me all that had happened upon his return. I was . . . unforgiving. He had consorts and concubines, to be sure, but they had arrived before I did. I was certain our private harmony mattered more than their public affections. Never did I imagine he could be seduced so easily. I withdrew my support and retreated to the Temple. He begged me to return but my heart had hardened. I had lost respect for him.

"By the next full moon, he was gone. A hunting mishap, they told me. I mourned, oh how I mourned! I never thought to not see him again . . .

"Three years later, a laughing monk in beggar's clothes passed through our Temple. He gave me one half of a silk fragment with these words threaded in gold. The other half, he told me, would reappear when I meet the son of my late sovereign. This son would be an only child who was the youngest of his siblings, a ruler of a Kingdom not his own, and a bearer of a legacy that he knew not. 'Then you will know,' the monk laughed hardest when he came to these words, 'what an illusion life is!'"

The Abbess pauses. She seems lost in thought, smoothing the folds of her robe. Shenya is sitting up now, trying to catch every word yet hardly believing any.

"What happened to his mother?" she manages at last.

"She retired to a nunnery, as did all Palace women once a new sovereign ascends to the Throne," the Abbess replies, almost absent-mindedly. With visible effort, she continues: "When your King Sihar gave me the other half of the *mantra*, I knew you two had a destiny together that could not be denied. So I persuaded you to enter his Palace, to advise him, to love him and be loved by him, for the time you had together."

"And what can I do with this memory, Learned One?" Shenya sobs bitterly.

"Cherish it and it will cherish you," the Abbess replies. "Not many in this world experience a grand passion, even with husbands and wives, children and comforts. We each have our *karma*, dear one, and its journeys are neither simple nor straightforward nor limited to our fragile sense of time."

Shenya listens to the Abbess and considers her words carefully, even long after she leaves. Lying there, in the dark, Shenya feels a release, finally. Her heart quiets and, that night, sleep enfolds her for the first time since leaving the Palace.

She has a dream.

> *She and Sihar are in a field of beautiful, large flowers – the size of elephants! Each flower opens with white petals, displaying red centers within. They are sitting under the Ancient One, by the bubbling brook, enjoying a simple but bounteous repast. Sihar drinks in her eyes and draws her close. "We are blessed," he smiles.*

Karma's Path

Years pass. King Sihar marries Queen Urma in the year of the Phoenix, a lucky omen. In due time, she bears him a son and a daughter. Both grow to be strong and handsome and quick. By rights as King, Sihar could have selected more wives or concubines, especially with only one son. But he chooses not to. Sihar honors this single marriage, even though it was forced on him. He needs no more.

Urma turns out to be a good wife and mother and Queen. Sihar's steadiness abates her suspicion and disdain of men. She grows to respect her husband, the King, and that leads to a kind of love that becomes, in time, more than what it was when they started. Like the orchid and the tree, a lack is turned into a talent that produces beautiful sprays. Urma's quick mind also helps Sihar rule wisely and astutely. They extend to each other a life of consideration, if not happiness.

Still, Urma notices, sometimes, when he thinks others are not watching, Sihar will stare out a window or search the starry sky above, as if waiting for something or someone. Other times, he will close his eyes and breathe in deeply whenever a westerly breeze brings an extra, special scent of mountain blooms. At such moments, his left hand will search for his rosary and rub the pearls, one by one, as if in prayer.

"Whereof your jade-and-ruby locket?" she asked him once.

"I gave it away," he answered simply. She didn't pursue it further.

In the thirtieth year of their union, Urma discovers she is dying of what the Tang doctors call "dry wind disease." Her condition worsens rapidly and, soon, she cannot leave her bed. On the morning of her celestial ascent, the Queen asks her husband for forgiveness.

"There is nothing to forgive," Sihar assures her kindly, holding her hands between his. "You have given me much, Urma, and I am very grateful."

Urma smiles at Sihar as a mother would to a child who has just fibbed.

"You have been good to me, my lord."

"And you to me, my dear," Sihar replies, not wishing to tax his wife further of her waning strength.

Urma closes her eyes, and peacefully enters the next world.

Norom is by Sihar's side when Urma passes. He has become a trusted friend, advisor, and beloved uncle to the Prince and the Princess. In Sihar and Vishaka, Norom finally finds a refuge. His affliction, no longer hidden, lessens in severity and frequency as a consequence.

On this day, a special memory comes upon him . . .

* * *

It was two years after the royal matrimony. He happened upon the Queen sitting by herself on a bench in the garden of roses and magnolia. She was crying. Norom aimed to turn away discreetly but his sleeve brushed against a thistle of roses. He could not free himself without drawing the Queen's attention. She looked up.

"Pardon, Your Highness," Norom apologized while disentangling his sleeve. He pretended not to notice Urma's tear-stained face and joked: "The rose, I'm afraid, it has caught me."

Urma's eyes brimmed anew.

"'Tis better caught than naught," she sobbed softly.

Norom rushed to her side, wrenched to see this proud, beautiful woman reduced to such helplessness and despair. He had heard the Court's malicious gossip: the King remained distant; for this reason, the Queen had yet to bear an heir for the Throne. *How many more years must the Kingdom endure?* tongues wagged.

"If I may . . ." Norom pulled a silk handkerchief from inside his robe. A grateful Urma took it since hers had long ago been drenched of use. He stood by quietly, awkwardly.

Urma finally spoke when she could: "We have burdened you, brother lord."

"Never, Your Highness!" Norom protested. He did not wish to intrude but neither could he ignore her need. "If I may be so bold, Your Highness, what could distress so?"

Urma sighed. It was uncharacteristic of her to be so open but she also found herself in an uncharacteristically difficult situation. And she knew Norom knew why since the whole Court knew.

"We've tried all ways yet remain exiled," she said as much as protocol allowed. She looked down. "Perhaps he cannot relent for his heart yearns for another."

Norom understood only too well.

"Perhaps, Your Highness . . ." he sat on a flat rock near her bench, searching for the right words, the right thoughts, ". . . one could take a pause, if only for a little while, and redirect one's energies elsewhere? Sometimes, the least direct route could take us to our destination far better than the most obvious one. 'Tis the surprise that makes the difference."

Urma looked at Norom.

"You are too kind, brother lord."

"Kindness, alas, has nothing to do with it, Your Highness. I myself have made the same mistake and too often in the past." Norom thought of Shenya. *Help me*, he prayed, *to help her – as you have helped me*. He ended up with a touch of comedy: "Even now, my surprise is a pinch in the arm to make sure I remember the lesson well."

Urma smiled, breaking through her tears. Seeing her recover even slightly heartened Norom. But Urma's visage darkened quickly as she whispered desperately: "What if he finds us . . . repugnant . . . for what we did?"

"No man could find you repugnant!" Norom protested without thinking. He seemed a dam suddenly released. "Your Highness is like the Sun and the Moon combined. You . . . *enthrall*."

Startled, Urma's eyes widened. Her lips parted but no words came out.

I've gone too far! Norom panicked. He groped for an explanation. "Beg your pardon, Your Highness, I . . . I . . ."

Instead, Urma placed a hand on his, as lightly and fleetingly as a butterfly visits a flower. Her voice and countenance were calm, even beatific.

"Thank you, brother lord, for you have given us more than what we deserve. Your wisdom comes from your heart. It will always stay near ours." And Urma left Norom sitting on the rock in the garden of roses and magnolia. They never spoke alone after that.

*   *   *

Indeed, Norom recalls on the day of her passing, the Queen made good on her promise. She devoted herself to charities and other good deeds, earning the King's respect that later turned into affection. It seemed as if they were meeting for the first time. Another year passed before the King approached his Queen, one balmy full moon's eve, and the Kingdom celebrated Prince Jandar's arrival nine moons later. *Farewell, my Queen, my Love,* Norom can now admit to himself.

Tandra, ever loyal, stays by Norom's side. But Tandra's artistry becomes so legendary that he is promoted to Master Royal Chef and many disciples follow him. Before each lesson, Tandra always burns incense in thanks to a Priestess who gave him his name.

By then, Mandu is long gone. When still alive, he was treated with grace and dignity, as the King's father-in-law. But Mandu never regained his former sense of self, so deep was his shame. He lived quietly, enjoying his grandchildren, until he, too, alighted to the heavens in his seventieth year.

Vishaka continues to prosper. Its relations with the Three Kings flourish. Water never becomes a problem again. Vishaka and its neighbors also begin to share more than water. The "Evening of Dreams" becomes a treasured tradition and is copied far and wide. Some dreams are performed time and again to popular demand, transforming them into myths. A favorite one has a giant bird swooshing down a village with a golden *sutra*.

Sihar never hears from Shenya again. Strict protocol prevents any contact between them, even through third parties. Although, decades later, when visiting dignitaries sometimes indulge in a cup or two too many, as they gossip into the night after one of Tandra's magical meals, they will let slip that a Priestess, famous for her knowledge of trees, has become the Abbess of the Temple of Knowledge. But they will quickly add that they are not sure, and will His Majesty please pardon their loose tongues, when catching sight of Norom's stern eye, realizing too late what they are saying and to whom. The Queen, they hear from the hallways, had banned a Temple Priestess from Vishaka long ago, due to some disagreement.

Freedom

After an appropriate period of mourning, Jandar and Salimar are invested as co-sovereigns of Vishaka. The people rejoice even as they sadden at Sihar's departure. But they understand. *He needs to grieve*, they sympathize. After all, he had only one Queen and she is gone.

On his first day of freedom, Sihar drives his chariot for a long ride. Duan is no more but his descendants populate the stables, the famous "sweating blood" spots a stamp of their lineage. One of them now brings Sihar to the forest. He has not been since . . . To Sihar's great delight, the Ancient One is still there! Just as twisted and black and magnificent as ever. And, as in the past, it hosts many a family of birds along with the bugs and the worms and, of course, an orchid or two. The brook remains, too, still bubbling alongside the Ancient One. *An eternal pair*, Sihar smiles to himself.

He wades into the brook for a refreshing wash . . . and encounters another man in the water. The hair is no longer so full or black. The moustache has grown into a full beard, flecked with white. A mature man of history now stands in place of that slim youth of old. Sihar chuckles and splashes the reflection, rippling it.

Tired, he sits down to rest, leaning against a large rock under a shading bush. Like second nature now, Sihar's left hand finds its way to the rosary, his fingers weaving through the pearls. Doing so always transports him somehow, as if winged by love's soft embrace. His eyes start to flutter. They feel heavy . . . as do the rest of his limbs . . .

A gurgle and a splash interrupt this idyll. Has he fallen asleep? Is he dreaming? With heart pounding and mind disbelieving, Sihar turns around, like that first time.

Shading his eyes from the setting sun, he makes out the shape of a woman approaching from the other side of the brook. Something flashes around her neck. It is a jade-and-ruby locket, looped in gold thread . . .

* * *

Alas, Gentle Friend, we must pause for now.
Dinner beckons to you and me both.

I hope you've enjoyed this tale as much
as I! We'll have many more, I promise.

Meanwhile, I bid you farewell – 'til next
we meet!

* * *

END OF BOOK I

Note

1   One cycle = 13 years.

BOOK II: THE LAUGHING MONK'S BET

* * *

Greetings, Gentle Friend! So good to see you again. How have you been? Well, I hope! From your smile, I see you are happy to see me again.

Sihar and Shenya, you ask, what's become of them? Ah, more wondrous tales await!

But first, how about some *chai*? Biscuits? Sit yourself down and . . . Yes, yes, I will get to the story . . . All good things in good time, Gentle Friend.

Comfortable? Now let's see . . . Where were they when we last met?

Ah, yes, by the Ancient One and the bubbling brook . . .

* * *

Thirty Years On

"Seems like *yesterday* we were sitting right here," Sihar laughs, pointing to the ground between his feet. He looks meaningfully at Shenya. "Nothing has changed."

Indeed, Time seems to have washed over her, leaving nary a trace. The Priestess remains as always: a lyrical spirit in flowing, white linen. Perhaps a slight fullness now pads the cheeks, a few more lines circle the eyes. Otherwise, Shenya is the same Priestess he met in this forest by this tree and its eternal partner, the bubbling brook, thirty years ago. Three tiers of black glory, each nestled within the other, still crown her atop. A strand of tiny, colorful beads wraps around each tier, rather than her pearls of old, now grasped in his left hand. They have stayed there every day since the moment she gave them to him.

"We were but children, then," she smiles for them both.

Much has happened since their first meeting at this very spot – but no nostalgia today! The moment is now and they savor it, drop by drop.

Shenya takes in the King. Sihar still manifests the sovereign and the man of yesteryear, commanding yet compassionate, noble and just. But she cannot ignore it: age has called on him. An undertow of Time has made its mark. It is not just the surface features that have grayed and creased. *His spirit*, she realizes. *It has carried too many burdens for too long*. Vishaka the Kingdom has benefited from his wise and vigilant rule. And Sihar the King is hailed far and wide. But what of Sihar the man, what lies ahead for him?

Of certainty, their love remains. It has nourished them through the peaks and valleys and sometimes underground burrows of a life fully lived. They have endured much and more is yet to come, Shenya feels sure. But will Time, that mercurial taskmaster, allow them to face it together?

* * *

Apologies, Gentle Friend, but I must interrupt. To truly understand the meaning of their happiness, this moment in their lives, we must turn to the story behind the story of Sihar and Shenya.

I know, I know. Trust me, you will cherish even more the sweetness and tenderness of this last episode by beginning at the beginning, when the Five Mythic Ones, on a hot and sultry day, bored with their usual distractions, encountered a laughing fool . . .

* * *

The Five Mythic Ones

"Oh," Love sighs, "I wish something exciting would happen!" A fine young tree, the Arboreal One rustles its leaves for effect, disturbing the round, pink buds from their sleep and sprinkling sweet dew all over. Power flames with irritation, swatting at the dew drops. Tiny yelps of steam seal their fate.

"Always pining away for something!" the Fiery One roars. Love gathers its evergreen branches and turns away with delicate disdain. *Brute!*

"You can't blame Love," Knowledge washes ashore diplomatically. "After all, excitement *is* exciting!" As usual, everyone ignores the Watery One. It's always swishing and splashing with one theory or another.

"I agree," Wealth chimes up uncharacteristically. A glittering, golden type and hard as they come, the Metallic One generally refrains from disclosing private thoughts or wasting time on chit-chat. But today, Wealth makes an unusual confession: "I, too, wish something would happen."

"Being *you* isn't rewarding enough?" Security chortles. The Earthy One finds this remark exceedingly funny. But no one else responds. Not even a peep. Each is miserable and determined to stay that way. Security harrumphs and digs further inside. *Typical*.

"Lo, there!" a friendly voice calls out. It's a religious pilgrim, a monk, in beggar's clothes and a laughing face. He carries a *thakum* walking stick, found only in the most sacred temples, and a large, round bowl, slightly chipped along the edge. "What ails thee on such a wondrous day?"

"We're bored," Love admits to the stranger.

Power denies it right away. "No, we're not! We're just . . ."

Security interrupts. "Who are you? Where did you come from and how did you get in *here*?"

The monk plunks down in front of the Five Mythic Ones, crossing his legs and setting his stick and bowl to one side.

"I come here often," he gleefully admits. "Usually, I play with your cousins Honor, Fear, Pleasure, and the others. Today, it is my great fortune – and perhaps yours –" he chuckles "– that we meet."

"Play?" Power takes a closer look at the monk, almost singeing his rags. "What do you mean by *that*?"

"Indeed," enjoins Knowledge, whose curiosity now rises to the fore. *This could be interesting.* The others regard the monk similarly.

"Let me ask you a question," the monk settles in. "Who amongst you, O Mythic Ones, is most *important* for happiness in the world?"

Power fires up first: "I, of course! Without Power, nothing happens."

"Nothing happens if there is *only* Power," Wealth objects with a clang, though making sure to keep a discreet distance. "Everyone would be afraid to say or do anything."

The others nod sagely. They have often felt the heat, if not the burn, of Power.

"I, on the other hand," Wealth broadcasts, "motivate everyone to seek more, achieve more, acquire more! I am an *inspiration*." Wealth's golden hue, already metallic in constitution, brightens even more at this declaration, threatening to blind all.

"You mean an *aspiration*," Security grumps, bringing everyone back to solid ground. "Without me, what good is Power or Wealth? Chaos and conflict would constantly besiege the world, thereby ruining it. Each would be at the other's throat, grabbing, stealing, and killing for that puny morsel of nothing before it is swallowed and digested, only to fight and struggle another day. Security provides the foundation that *makes* Power and Wealth." The Earthy One concludes with a satisfied *clump*.

"How boring!" Love protests ardently. The Arboreal One sways alluringly. "Love is what gives the fun and fizz to *having* Power, Wealth, and Security! Why bother otherwise?" Love shakes its leaves and buds, sprinkling more dew everywhere, instantly sprouting greens and fragrances wherever it drops. Love is especially pleased with itself.

Knowledge speaks last. An intellectual, Knowledge always likes to soak in what others have to say before revealing itself.

"Indeed," Knowledge laps smoothly, like a gentle wave on a stretch of moonlit beach. "Why bother to pursue Power, Wealth, Security, and even Love if, at the end of the day, there is no *meaning* to any of it?"

The others stare blankly at Knowledge. *What is this slippery character up to?*

"But," Knowledge flows on calmly, used to the others not perceiving its depth, "I won't. For I know this mirthful soul here –" Knowledge gestures to the Laughing Monk "– is playing a trick on us."

"Trick?!" Power blazes redly in the middle and whitely at the tips. "How *dare* you?!"

"Only a beggar would do something like this," Wealth sniffs.

"Who let him in anyway?" Security demands.

"Pity," Love sighs again. "I was beginning to like him."

"Wait!" Knowledge exhorts. "The trick is for us to recognize that we are *all* important for happiness in the world."

Oh, the others chorus in one, tadly sheepish voice. The Laughing Monk cannot stop laughing.

"O Mythic Ones," he manages to catch a breath. "You are too charming! Would you like to play more with me?"

"*More*?" ignites Power.

"With *you*?" pounds Security.

"What's in it for us?" hammers Wealth.

"*Us*?" flutters Love.

"How?!" splashes Knowledge.

"What if," the monk proposes, "we raise the stakes by asking: Which *combination* of Power, Wealth, Security, Love, and Knowledge would provide the greatest happiness?"

"Raise the stakes?" Power flares again. "What kind of nonsense is that?!"

"Really," Love dismisses. "You're all smoke! I, for one, would *love* to play."

Wealth agrees: "After all, what's there to lose?"

Yes, the others echo. Let's play! And Power grudgingly concedes: "Oh, alright."

The Laughing Monk rubs his hands. "Now let me take your bets."

The Mythic Ones retreat to a corner to confer. They soon re-emerge.

"We bet the winning combination is Power and Wealth!" Power and Wealth crow.

"We bet on Love and Security!" Love and Security cling to each other happily.

"And I bet on myself as the key to Power and Wealth, Love and Security!" Knowledge spouts smugly.

The Laughing Monk congratulates the Mythic Ones, then asks: "How shall we play these bets?"

"I know!" Love waves enthusiastically, fluttering its leaves. "Let's have a love story in a beautiful, lush setting. There's nothing more compelling than romance in paradise –"

Power's flame dims. "Please, no sappy, soppy, simpering love story! We have enough of those."

"A love story is fine," intercedes Knowledge, who's always skeptical of, yet strangely attracted to Love. "We'll make it full of plots and schemes to satisfy Power here."

The Fiery One's blaze returns.

"The story must have substance, something to grab onto," Security intones. "It must be grounded in what's real. No up-in-the-air abstractions for me, thank you very much." Security throws a dirty look at Knowledge. *You know what I mean.*

"Whatever it is," Wealth adds breathlessly, surprising all who are more used to its monochromatic humor, "we must have lots and lots of it!"

"We shall have a Court," Knowledge swells with intrigue, "in an ancient and glorious Kingdom!" Knowledge looks askance at Wealth. *It's always missing the point!*

"Most worthy." The monk bows in appreciation to the Mythic Ones. "Now that we know what kind of story we'll be playing and the setting, who should we have for the players?"

The Mythic Ones sink into silence. Suddenly, they begin to argue and shout, point and stomp. The Laughing Monk observes them calmly. *They'll sort it out*, he knows. And, indeed, they do.

"We've got it!" Security calls out, raising little balls of dust as it does.

"It's not perfect," Love blooms, "but we like it."

Wealth and Knowledge concur. Only Power hesitates.

"I don't know . . . "

"Come on," they cajole, "playing this game is not undignified."

Knowledge hits upon the winning argument, stamping out any doubt in the Fiery One: "Who knows? You may well end up the winner!"

Power lights up.

The Laughing Monk turns to the Mythic Ones and smiles: "What now?"

The Human World

"Let us enter the Human World," Knowledge suggests. "It bears the greatest unpredictability and, therefore, the greatest fun."

"The Human World," Security reminds everyone, "is also the most concrete. Not only is it built on dirt and rocks, wind and rain, but its inhabitants also require these for their daily survival."

Wealth glows with anticipation. "There is much to be had there . . ."

"And for this reason," Power warms to the subject, "humans are consumed with power . . ."

"Let us not forget –" Love taps its branches to rouse Power and Wealth from their musings "– humans take bodily form. We must do so, too, if we are to play this game."

Excellent! the Mythic Ones exclaim. They haven't taken bodily form in a long while.

"I shall be a Ruler!" Power announces.

"And I, a General!" Security follows.

"I will be a Scholar, of course," Knowledge humbly submits.

"And I," Love declares with flourish, "will be a Poet!"

Hm, Knowledge thinks, *an unexpected choice. Perhaps there is more to Love than it seems.*

Wealth, though, cannot decide.

"I don't know what form to take," the Metallic One complains.

"How about a Merchant?" Security proposes. "They usually amass a lot of wealth."

"Too mundane," Wealth rejects.

"A sweaty slave, then!" Love suggests eagerly.

"How is a slave *wealth*?!" challenges Power. *Love can be so silly!*

"A slave makes wealth possible," Love rebuts Power smartly.

Hm, Knowledge appreciates again, *not bad*.

"No, no," Wealth dismisses, feeling increasingly forlorn. "A slave is too tragic."

"Since our story is located in a Kingdom . . ." Knowledge begins.

"A Treasurer!" Power billows with self-satisfaction. "That's what you should be. Every Ruler needs a Treasurer."

Wealth brightens at first, then darkens into doom again.

"I want to *be* Wealth, not just in charge of it," the Metallic One grouses. "A Ruler *embodies* Power, just like a General *is* Security itself. The same is true for a Poet and Love, a Scholar and Knowledge."

"How about," the Laughing Monk suggests, "if we borrow an expression from the Han?"

"What do you mean?" the Mythic Ones ask all at once.

"The Han have a saying: 'A daughter is like a thousand pieces of gold'," the Laughing Monk replies. "So maybe you could be a daughter?"

A golden hue returns immediately to the Metallic One.

"Yes, that's it!"

And the Laughing Monk, along with the Mythic Ones, hops on one leg then the next. The game is about to begin!

"But wait!" Love cries out. "We haven't selected our bodies yet!"

Everyone pauses, momentarily stumped.

"You start," Knowledge drips.

"Alright," Love begins to ruminate. "Since I've decided to be a Poet . . . I'll take the form of a handsome young man! I will call him Rashis."

Hm, Knowledge notes a third time.

"A General is a man, of course," Security proclaims. "A well-seasoned man. General Onor, he is."

"I will take the form of a male scholar, a Counselor to the Court," Knowledge states. "His name is Drat'n."

What airs! Wealth mocks.

"Since I am a Ruler," Power flames majestically, "I shall be a King."

"Same old, same old!" Love pouts. "Why not change the usual and be a Queen?"

"Yes," Wealth clinks merrily. "Let us be sisters. Power and Wealth are usually related. You are Queen Rima and I, Yna, your younger sister!"

"Alright," Power concedes again. *It makes little difference,* Power shrugs. *After all, power is power.*

"This will make things interesting, indeed," comments Knowledge.

The Laughing Monk steps in. "We now have the story, the setting, and the players. Shall we throw them together and see what turns out?"

Yes, yes! the Mythic Ones agree. And they meld earth with water, metal and wood, and fire them into tiny figurines, each representing the human forms of the Five Mythic Ones: Queen Rima for the Fiery One of Power, Princess Yna for the Metallic One of Wealth, General Onor for the Earthy One of Security, Counselor Drat'n for the Watery One of Knowledge, and Rashis the Poet for the Arboreal One of Love.

After admiring their fine handiwork, the Mythic Ones are ready to throw the figurines into the Human World when, suddenly, the Laughing Monk raises a bony hand:

"What about the bet?"

The Bet

Oh yes, the bet! In their excitement, the Mythic Ones had forgotten all about it.

"Throw your challenge, Pilgrim," Power commands.

"The bet is," the monk offers jovially, "even if you win, you lose."

Indignation explodes all around. "Impossible!" "Outrageous!" "Ridiculous!" "What?"

All, that is, except for Knowledge. The Watery One slides up to the Laughing Monk and asks: "What do you mean?"

The Laughing Monk recites in a singsong voice:

> *"Power more is power less,*
> *Wealth finds not in what's possess'd.*
> *Security seeks strength but quakes, instead;*
> *Love fans all except the head.*
> *And Knowledge knows much yet realizes little,*
> *Forever missing the sacred middle!"*

The Mythic Ones are stunned into silence. Never before have they encountered a rhyming bet! The Metallic One speaks first.

"What do we get if we win?"

"Whatever you wish," answers the Laughing Monk.

"And what if you win?" Power asks.

"Whatever *I* wish!" the monk replies, laughing harder.

The Mythic Ones agree. It seems like a fair bet. *After all*, Wealth smirks on the side, *it's five against one!*

"Let's play!" Love prompts.

"Let me offer my services," Knowledge glides graciously toward the center of the group. The Watery One expands into a large, dark pool. "We can see how our human selves will fare through this reflection."

The Mythic Ones throw in their figurines. And they gather round to watch . . .

The Proposal

"Sister," Princess Yna addresses Queen Rima with a quick curtsy, "what darkens your brow?" Yna enters Rima's chamber for their usual afternoon treat of jasmine tea with peeled lychees in coconut water. A red-beaked parrot of brilliant-blue wings and a golden orange breast sits atop her shoulder. "*Brow!*" it caws. Yna gives it a sunflower seed from an inside pouch to reward the bird. Rima pauses to smile at her younger sister's fondness for all creatures, big and small. But the Queen cannot indulge in such sentiments today. A far weightier matter awaits her. Rima sighs deeply and walks to the window.

"A messenger has arrived from King Farhad."

"The Conqueror?" Yna gasps, looking up with excitement, disturbing Caw-Caw. It flies indignantly to a wooden perch nearby, on which hang Rima's royal silks.

"The same," Rima affirms, so distracted she forgets, as usual, to shoo the parrot from her robes. "The Conqueror has proposed marriage."

"Sister!" exclaims Yna, clapping her hands. "What an honor for our house!" ("*Honor!*" Caw-Caw repeats, flapping its wings.) The prospect of a royal wedding instantly fills her head with Romance, Love, Banquets, Music, handsome princes . . .

"Calm, Bina," Rima interrupts, using Yna's childhood name, her cheeks darkening further with impatience. "Marriage is but one way for the Conqueror to achieve his real desire: Vayanak. Our land enjoys the sea on three sides. Farhad's empire may be vast but it is mostly dry. He needs the life-giving circulations of our sea for commerce and trade. That would enrich his nobles. His shares and crops would also harvest well from our irrigations. That would enrich his farmers. And his soldiers would benefit from both. Otherwise, Farhad is too vulnerable to a siege." Rima is well schooled in the politics of power.

Yna nods thoughtfully. She bears no ill-will to Rima for bursting her fantasy with reality. After all, she *is* the Queen.

"An alliance," Yna suggests helpfully, "would surely enhance our Royal House. Why, then, the shadows on your face?"

"I suppose I am of age," Rima sighs again. "I cannot expect to sit on the Throne for-ever without a consort. But I feel not yet ready somehow . . ." Rima's voice trails off.

Yna notices her sister's coloring shading into translucence, indicating deep dis-quiet. The younger instantly regrets her lack of consideration for the older. Yna approaches Rima and embraces her fondly.

"Ah, Sister, when is one ever ready? Though you have governed ably since Mother and Father passed, and we were but children then, you deserve to unburden yourself to someone close to your heart."

"Only with the great help of General Onor have we managed to stay on the Throne," Rima recalls loyally, reverting unconsciously to royal speech. "Still," she adds wistfully, now speaking in her own voice and referring to King Farhad, "will he be close to my heart?"

Rima blushes at her own thoughts. The Palace brought up the Princesses with the strictest protocol, allowing only women, relatives, and eunuchs on the premises. Rima may be Queen – she ascended to the Throne when the King and Queen died in an unforeseen boating mishap a cycle ago[1] – but the two royal heirs remain insulated from the normal affairs of young people their age. This hasn't stopped them, however, from developing a vivid imagination, especially in Yna.

"I'm sure King Farhad's courier brought a likeness of His Majesty," Yna brightens. "Perhaps his person will move you!"

Rima points to her mahogany bed where lies a scroll of smashed cowrie shells. Flattened and glazed, the shells make a costly writing tablet and, in this case, a portrait canvas. It aims to impress and does so. Only someone like the Conqueror could afford such an expense in material and labor. Yna quickly strides over and picks up the heavy and unwieldy scroll. She unrolls it carefully to inspect the image inside.

"Well," Yna peers at the scroll, "he seems big and strong. Truly a conqueror. It's harder to judge his face . . . The drawing is not very good." She refrains from mentioning that the portrait, despite all intents, reveals the Conqueror as a man at least twice Rima's age. But the Queen knows her sister too well not to catch the subterfuge.

"His visage matters less than his vision," Rima redirects their talk. "Will he accept me as his co-sovereign or will he take supremacy as my lord and master? I cannot think of only myself in this matter. It concerns our Kingdom and our people as well."

"Let us not judge in haste, Sister," Yna advises. Her fertile mind includes, strangely, a strain of the practical. "As the Kingdom's Treasurer, let me suggest we invite His Majesty to a royal feast, so the two sovereigns can meet – without saying 'Yay' or 'Nay', of course."

Rima's mood lightens, her coloring returns to its usually healthy hue.

"Yes, Bina," she answers, "you always have the best ideas. Let us inform General Onor."

"But first, Sister," Yna reminds Rima, "let us enjoy our afternoon treat!" And the two, Queen and Treasurer, link arms to sit down and partake of their tea and lychees, while giggling like the sisters that they are. And Caw-Caw flies happily back onto Yna's shoulder.

"*Enjoy!*" the bird barks.

The Invitation

After half a moon, a courier brings the Royal Invitation from Vayanak. It is written on a scroll of square plates made of mother-o'-pearl. Each square is pierced and chained to the others with a tiny, conch-like brass coil whose spout is sealed by a single bud of juniper. Precious spring water inside each coil nourishes the bud to perfume during the long trip to the Conqueror. Light and delicate, Vayanak's Invitation unfurls to thrice the length of the Conqueror's, temporarily blinding all with its brilliance.

The Invitation begins with Queen Rima thanking His Majesty King Farhad for asking after her health. In turn, the Invitation wishes the best for His Majesty's constitution:

"May Your Breath cover the four seas, Your Spirit soar beyond the clouds, Your Smile illuminate the evening sky, and Your Vision warm the world like the rays of the morning sun," so on and so forth. Halfway down does the scroll come to its actual message:

"Queen Rima welcomes His Majesty King Farhad, Victorious Conqueror of the Seven Realms, Noble Emperor on the Peacock Throne, and Illustrious Founder of the Gorgeon Dynasty, to visit the fair Kingdom of Vayanak, at His Majesty's royal leisure, knowing the burdens of Empire, the vagaries of the Elements, the grandness of his

Entourage," so on and so forth. Not a word is mentioned of the proposal.

Neither the message on the scroll – nor the scroll itself – is lost on the Conqueror.

"They aim to put us off!" he roars as Counselor Drat'n reads the Invitation. "They think they're too good for us!"

King Farhad is a powerfully built man two cycles senior to Rima. Blessed with a magnificent, full beard, now dappled with light amid the dark, Farhad looks every inch the daunting Conqueror. "That pipsqueak-of-a-queen dares to treat us like some flush-faced, slaveboy-in-love! Our army could crush her Kingdom in the blink of an eye!" Farhad pounds his iron fist on the golden arm of the Peacock Throne, upsetting a goblet of wine nearby.

Counselor Drat'n lowers the scroll. A slight man of meticulous countenance and manner, he is as perceptive as he is precise. Still young enough to chase after ambition, the Counselor is, nonetheless, old enough to perceive the ways of the world. Both men know the King's proposal of marriage is but a courtesy. Both also know that it is always better to win through seduction than conquest. Why waste precious men, horses, and elephants? The Empire needs them all.

More than this, the Empire needs what Vayanak alone can provide: culture. It would deliver the imperial in the Empire. Swords and arrows may submit the people to

Farhad's conquest but only culture can win them to his *rule*. Otherwise, he will find himself constantly fighting discontent from within. Even if he could pacify these rebellions, a dynasty without culture cannot last beyond its founder and maybe one heir. Who would sing his praises, then, or pray for his protection? How would children a hundred – nay, a thousand – harvests hence remember him? Where lies the victory in *that*?

Yet culture is not something he can simply command or install. A delicate, elusive creature of ancient and noble lineage, culture must come to *him* and preferably with a smile. Only then would the people agree to live, labor, and war for the Empire. For all this, the Conqueror needs the Kingdom of Vayanak. Because of its circulations of the sea, Vayanak dazzles as the most brilliant gem of culture throughout the known world. And the peak of Vayanak's gem is its Queen.

"Sire," Drat'n addresses the Conqueror, full of reason as usual, "the Invitation may offend in what it fails to address. Nevertheless, the Invitation still invites."

The Conqueror looks at his Counselor. *No doubt*, Farhad notes to himself, *the fellow's clever*.

Knowing his sovereign, Counselor Drat'n adds: "Why not venture to Vayanak and meet with the Queen? She may be beautiful or distasteful, one will certainly find out."

"Oh she's beautiful, alright," Farhad assures his Chief Counselor. "Word has it that the Queen blooms like a hibiscus in Summer and her sister, the Kingdom's Treasurer, shimmers like the morning dew." The Conqueror snorts. "What strange customs these people have, putting women in charge! Perhaps we should betroth ourselves to both and double our fortune!"

King and Counselor share a hearty laugh.

Indeed, why not? Drat'n thinks. Women like Queen Rima and her sister are to be had by men like King Farhad. *Still*, the Counselor's inner voice cautions, *let us not assume too much.*

"I have heard the young Queen is fond of word-songs," Drat'n suggests as he rolls up the Invitation. "Perhaps we could bring Rashis the Poet. Once they know what luminous talent bedecks Your Majesty's realm, Queen Rima and her Court could not but yield."

"Excellent," the Conqueror nods. He has seen how the Court's ladies swoon to Rashis's word-songs . . . "Prepare our response!" The Conqueror smiles knowingly at his Counselor: "Our latest victories in war afford us some patience in peace, eh?"

We are delighted to accept, the scribe chisels dutifully, so on and so forth.

The Reply

"He arrives in three moons!" Rima drops Farhad's scroll, letting it roll noisily and unceremoniously on the marble floor. *So soon!*

Yna picks up the scroll and scans it quickly. She must start preparations straight away.

Frenzy races throughout the Palace. Much needs to be done: the loveliest orchids cultivated so they can be cut and placed in small pools with candles on the day of his arrival, special incense rolled and dried so it can perfume the air with just the right balance of piety and graciousness, musicians rehearsed and ready to play, and, of course, the welcoming feast. Pigs must feed extra now to ready them for slaughter in three moons hence; fowls cleaned and fluffed for easy plucking later; rods and nets repaired to haul fresh catch; rabbits caught and husbanded. The gardens and nurseries also need extra priming to coax vegetables and fruits, berries and nuts, into their most glorious, tastiest display. Not to mention, the Palace and its grounds need additional arrangements, to showcase its best, inside and out. An endless list of chores! *Really*, Yna thinks disapprovingly, *the Conqueror could be more considerate.*

Meanwhile, Queen Rima holds counsel with her former Regent, General Onor. A man much like her father, the General has aided and shielded Rima since her ascension at the tender age of seven. Yna, two years younger, cried every night from one full moon to the next until General Onor brought, one day, a furry hopper with big ears for the little one. Ever since, Yna finds herself in all creatures she could feed, pet, cradle, brush, or ride and they, in turn, share with her all their love and devotion.

Back then, Rima herself could not stop trembling as soon as the sun fell behind the Palace walls. *What will happen to us without Father-King and Mother-Queen?* She sucked her thumb furiously every night. Her uncles quarreled loudly and constantly, even before bidding farewell to her parents' earthly forms. Red rashes started to plague her neck and hands. No doctor or medicine could cure her. But these died down as the harvests passed and General Onor proved steadfast in his protection of the Princesses, never allowing anything or anyone to come close to harming them. Rima knew not when, but her uncles soon stopped quarreling as each became governor of a frontier province. Rima knows how much she owes the General and trusts him implicitly.

The General knows, too. Without him, Vayanak's bickering factions would have destroyed the Kingdom, devastating one and all. Moreover, he has come to love the two little girls like his own. He would do anything for them.

"What say you to this proposal, General?" she asks. They are in the General's special greeting room, darkened by rosewood shutters of intricate latticework to shield against the bright sunlight yet allow in the cooling drafts. The General uses this room whenever his affliction strikes. It has lessened slightly in recent years but the piercing pain in his left eye still attacks now and then, and for no apparent reason.

General Onor leans heavily on the right arm of his rattan couch. His left hand comforts the aching eye with a hot towel. Large, silk pillows prop from behind as he sits cross-legged on the couch. Young attendants fan him rhythmically from behind with large, peacock feathers. Children of the older maids, their sole duty is to fan Grandfather General when ill.

Rima consults General Onor from a large, rattan chair with a rounded back like embracing wings. Placed to the General's right line of sight, the seating relieves his left. Rima's slippered feet rest on a black, wooden stool, carved like a half papaya and oiled with eucalyptus sap to ensure fragrant conversations. Beside the Queen is a delicate cup of tea, sitting quietly on a slim, tall side-table of lacquered teak. Taking a sip, Rima steals a glance at her old mentor with sympathy and concern. *He has worked too hard for us and the Kingdom*, she chides herself. Despite his ailment, Onor the General remains, as always, sharp-minded and plain-spoken.

"It could be a worthy match, Your Highness," he answers slowly. "King Farhad has become sovereign of the largest stretch of known territory since his many victories. As his consort, you would greatly enhance Vayanak."

"But could Vayanak be swallowed by his empire?" Rima presses gently, sensitive to his condition.

"That is a tricky question, Your Highness." General Onor hands the towel to an attendant.

Another appears with a tray of dark sandalwood. On it are laid two porcelain bowls of ox-blood red, inlaid with delicately carved ivory flowers trailed by winding stems and curly leaves. A matching spoon rests inside each bowl. From one steams the hot, milky soup of ground almonds sweetened with sugarcane, the only sustenance the General can down at times like these. The other bowl also holds a sweet soup but it is of wild white fungus mixed with lotus seeds. The General knows the Queen dislikes almonds.

"To refuse would be to offend," Onor continues while spooning the milk to cool it, "in which case he might attack and annex us anyway." The old Regent has never spared the truth to Rima, having faith in her innate intelligence and character, even when she should have been chasing butterflies in the garden instead of learning about statecraft at his knee.

"So there is no possibility of refusing . . .?"

"There may be, however," the General suggests, "a way of accepting." His tone lightens at the thought of strategy. He takes one swallow of the almond soup then sets it aside on the couch.

He's feeling better, Rima can tell.

"That is . . .?"

The General signals the attendants to leave. The pain in his eye has abated with the hot towel and sweet soup. More importantly, he doesn't want little ears to tell big stories.

"We could make him so enamored of Your Highness that he would concede to your every wish," the General suggests directly. Never in his wildest dreams did General Onor ever imagine, as Master Strategist and Royal Regent, he would have to counsel the Queen on romance one day. But here they are.

Rima leans in, and the General proceeds: "Of course, Your Highness has youth and beauty and that would captivate any man. But Farhad is a seasoned sovereign. He has seen his share of pleasure. It is rumored he has sired a child in every territory he has captured. He takes women as a prize of war. This is the first time he has formally sought a consort." The old General pauses for Rima to take in the full meaning of this statement. She does. "To capture his attention and *keep* it," the General continues, "Your Highness will have to take extra measures."

Rima's heart jumps, her scalp begins to burn. *What foul perversities must I endure?!*

"I have heard," the General's voice reaches her as though from a distance, "King

Farhad favors word-songs even though he himself, due to the hardships of war, cannot read or write. One of his most valued attendants, for example, is a poet."

"Oh!" Rima exhales with relief, her scalp cooling. She can handle word-songs. The Queen picks up her bowl of fungus and seeds and takes a satisfying taste. "You always have the best soups," she compliments the General.

The Arrival

As promised, King Farhad arrives at the outskirts of Vayanak in three moons' time. A courier runs ahead to announce his presence.

Along with the best of his military, mounted on horses, camels, and elephants, Farhad travels with another army of attendants, cooks, translators, scribes, painters, and entertainers. Six large carts carry precious gifts for the Queen and her Kingdom: glass beads and cups; rose water; olives, figs, and pomegranates; rare spices like nutmeg, black pepper, cardamom, caraway, and aniseed; and even rarer items like frankincense, myrrh, and gum. Farhad the Suitor would not second Farhad the Conqueror!

One carriage behind the King rides Counselor Drat'n. Instead of silk pillows and other comforts, as in the King's chariot, scrolls of powdered palm leaf surround the Counselor. Less cumbersome and definitely less costly than smashed cowrie shells, these palm leaf scrolls serve well enough for daily administration. Although they need constant powdering with the ashes of black tea leaves to keep away hungry mites. (Consequently, yellow-stained fingers signal high office.) The scrolls sit in piles, waiting for the Counselor to decide which ones to read to the Conqueror, which not. Drat'n's candle often burns late into night. His station brings much power but also much burden. One cannot do without the other.

Rashis the Poet rides behind on his steed, trotting along with the other high-level attendants. Rashis much prefers the fresh, open air to any enclosed chariot no matter how fancy. As the Conqueror's Head Scribe of Word-Songs, Rashis would, in any case, accompany His Majesty on a social outing. But Rashis knows he has a special mission this time: to woo the Queen of Vayanak and her Court for his sovereign. Not only is the Queen beautiful, he has heard, but she is also expert at word-songs. *A double challenge*, he smiles to himself.

A man of unusual beauty and talent, Rashis seems loved by all. Tall enough to inspire a young girl's shy glances, he is not so tall she must crane her neck. Strong enough to climb a pole wet with mud during the spring festivals, he does not, at the same time, bulge with unsightly brawn. And sensitive enough to rouse a fluttering of hearts even in well-married ladies, Rashis remains a welcome fellow to hunting and drinking games with his peers. No question, Rashis beguiles from the curly black hair that dances nimbly atop to a pair of perfectly shaped, muscular legs that show to pleasing advantage especially when, as now, they are let loose in a riding tunic. Many a court lady has lost her heart to this enticing elixir of a man – and he knows it. *What new beauties await . . .?* Rashis muses. Suddenly, he is reminded of a certain noblewoman who has become too attentive of late. *Yes*, Rashis decides, *this new outing comes at a good time!*

In Preparation

King Farhad and his retinue enter the Palace grounds a fortnight later, when the sun falls midway to dusk. Attendants rush over to lead the visitors to their quarters in a side garden, reserved for guests only.

Farhad washes off the dust and fatigue of travel from large bowls decorated in the ancient style of black ash and wood, found only in Vayanak. Cool, spring water invites from within, sprinkled with petals of marigold. *Vayanakans know their refinements*, he appreciates.

Drying off with a white muslin towel, Farhad takes in the sight of the Palace from his window and marvels at its strangeness. A towering structure of gold, marble, and teak, sitting majestically atop a mountain ringed by swirling mist, the Palace surveys all throughout the Kingdom. *Truly,* the Conqueror acknowledges, *it is a haven for the gods!*

That evening, King Farhad and his men are in the Great Hall ready to be presented to Her Highness, Queen Rima, and her Court. Finery bedecks all: King Farhad, imposing in his royal silks, glittering jewels, and a gleaming, silver dagger tucked in a belt of wizened leather; Counselor Drat'n, somber and dignified in darker, more austere hues; and Rashis the Poet, dashing even in his simple attendant's wear.

They await with bated breath (even the Conqueror!) as the Great Hall's giant mahogany doors slide slowly apart. Attendants on each side swing large, brass bells to announce with grave ceremony the entrance of His Majesty King Farhad, Victorious Conqueror of the Seven Realms, Noble Emperor on the Peacock Throne, Illustrious Founder of the Gorgeon Dynasty, so on and so forth.

The Welcome

A cavernous space opens before them. Doves flap in the air, so high is the ceiling. It bears a frieze chiseled in teak, sandalwood, and gold, telling of Vayanak's gods and goddesses at play, at work, at war.

This pantheon of the heavens tops four marble pillars, twined in purple bougainvillea. Without walls, the Hall breathes gingerly with sheer, long panels of chiffon the color of the sea in tranquility. Their undulations reveal sets of musicians playing on reed instruments in a garden thick with jasmine and gardenia, lavender and mimosa. Aromatic incense fills the Hall; its smokiness enhanced by a thousand specks of candlelight in pools of floating orchids, on low-lying tables, even on the marble floor to help direct guests.

All of Vayanak's Court is gathered in the Hall. They bow welcomes with smiling faces and folded hands, wearing silks and feathers, rubies and pearls amidst statues of sandstone and lime.

Queen Rima heads the Court. A golden headdress of sparkling spikes, each encrusted with precious stones, crowns her atop. Though proper and discreet, the Queen's gown of golden silk mesh cannot hide the young womanhood ripening underneath. *More than a hibiscus in bloom*, the Conqueror admires, *she is, impossibly, the sun and the moon combined!* On each side of the Queen, at one step below, stand General Onor and Princess Yna. Full military regalia adorn the General. Princess Yna sparkles in silver to her sister's gold. Her headdress rises in three round balls, like shells from the sea, each one smaller than the other until it concludes in a long, sharp peak.

The Conqueror straightens his shoulders and juts out his chin. In all his years of war and conquest, victory and supremacy, he has never before seen the beauty and grandness of what appears before him now. *Let me not gape*, he reminds himself, *like a country bumpkin's first visit to the capital*. He strides forward purposefully. Counselor Drat'n and Rashis the Poet follow behind at a respectful pace.

"Welcome, brother lord," Queen Rima gestures to the seating next to hers but it still rests at a respectful distance apart.

"Health and Happiness to you, madam," King Farhad bows with folded hands.

He steps up to the dais and both discover, to each other's secret dismay, that the Queen stands a full head taller than the Conqueror. But neither reveals any inner feelings. Each maintains the required decorum. They sit down, indicating to the gathering that they, too, may take their seats. General Onor invites Counselor Drat'n to settle near him. Rashis the Poet stays several rungs below with the rest of the attendants. A gong sounds and the feast begins.

Stratagems

The festivities last five days and five nights. Each day bears a different theme: histories of Vayanak's noble kings and queens, the courage and accomplishments of its people, lyrical songs, fairy dances, mythical tales – with more to follow; each night, a sample of Vayanak's unique sea and forest cuisine. The Court bestows a plentitude of food, drink, theater, manners, and other artful refinements onto the Conqueror and his party – everything except an opportunity to broker the purpose of his visit.

"Have you approached the General?" King Farhad inquires testily of his Counselor on the sixth day, when the Palace has graciously allowed a temporary pause in the feasting, upon the visiting sovereign's request. Indeed, Farhad is overwhelmed. He lies sprawled on his rattan couch with a cool muslin towel over his eyes. Hospitality has defeated the Conqueror where no army in the known world could: his stomach. Used to the simple rations of military campaigns, the Conqueror cannot take to the fancy fineries of cultured cuisine. He must rest – and plot.

During the feasts, he sits next to Queen Rima on the dais but royal protocol prohibits any serious talk. The distance between their tables also makes any conversation between them impossible without resorting to an embarrassment of shouts. Farhad knows Drat'n suffers the same fate with Onor but wonders whether the Counselor has succeeded in catching the General alone.

"Alas, nay, Sire," Drat'n replies with a regretful bow. "I have not been able to ask if, not to mention when, we could discuss the matter at hand."

"These Vayanakans," the Conqueror growls, "they are not easy!" He sits up, letting the towel fall to one side. "Any recommendations, Counselor?"

Drat'n looks down thoughtfully. "Perhaps, Sire," he begins, "we could try a counter-stratagem . . .?"

"Go on."

The Counselor continues more forthrightly. "Let us request a small gathering here, at our guest quarters, to declare our humble gratitude at Vayanak's grand generosity and benevolence. We will invite only their Royal Highnesses and the General. We have enough attendants in tow to take care of the rest."

"Our venue?" asks Farhad, intrigued by how Drat'n's mind can shift so fluidly from the military to the social arts.

"Word-songs."

"Ah! We were wondering when the Poet would come of use."

"Your humble servant had thought of presenting him at one of the feasts. But they are much too big with too many in attendance. A smaller gathering might be more, shall we say, appropriate?"

The Conqueror grunts a contented reply and lies back down on the couch, returning the muslin towel to his eyes.

Meanwhile, Queen Rima and Princess Yna are also in conference with their advisor, General Onor.

"We cannot stall forever, General," Rima frets. Onor looks upon the Queen kindly. *Such heavy burdens for one so young*, he sympathizes. *But that is her* karma.

"I agree, Your Highness." The old Regent bows. He hesitates slightly before asking: "Forgive my intrusion but . . . how does Your Highness regard the Conqueror?"

"I – We – don't . . . can't . . . really . . ."

Yna sees her sister struggling, patches of red blotching her neck and hands. The younger quickly intervenes on behalf of the older.

"The Queen cannot decide as yet. She needs more time and exposure."

General Onor bows in acknowledgment.

"We see too much of the Conqueror and not enough of the man," Rima finally finds the right words.

"I recommend, then," the old Regent advises, "that we do nothing. Let us see how King Farhad responds. What he proposes next will give us a measure of the man, not just the Conqueror." *She must go to him willingly,* Onor knows, *if this union is to succeed.*

The two sisters feel most assured by the General's wise counsel. *Yes*, they nod to each other, *let us wait.*

Another Invitation

Counselor Drat'n appears before Her Highness Queen Rima as he has done every morning since the Conqueror's arrival. King Farhad always extends his greetings to Her Highness through his Counselor, as a matter of course. But this morning, Drat'n has another message to deliver.

"His Majesty King Farhad begs an indulgence, Your Highness," the Counselor declares, surprising one and all. "He requests permission to reciprocate Vayanak's grand hospitality with a modest, little repast for Your Highness and Princess Yna, as well as General Onor, of course, on the next full moon at our quarters." The Counselor bows respectfully in the General's direction. The General returns the courtesy.

Rima steals a glance at her former Regent. Though he makes nary a move, the General's eyes advise silently yet clearly: *To refuse would be to insult, and we cannot afford to insult.* Rima understands all too well. She turns to Drat'n with a beatific smile: "We are most honored, Counselor. Please extend our delight and our thanks to His Majesty."

Drat'n bows deeply as the Queen rises and departs from her morning council.

An Evening of Word-Songs

Farhad's attendants work furiously to prepare for the royal visit. Though they make a valiant effort and produce the best they can for the occasion, it cannot, of course, compare with Vayanak's royal feasts. *Still*, Yna notes to herself, as they enter the guest quarters, *they've made pleasant arrangements*.

Instead of tiny candles everywhere, as would be Vayanak's custom, flaming torches head bamboo poles staked into the ground, creating a path, then a circle, for the guests. Counselor Drat'n has chosen an exquisite, small garden for the repast. *Dhatura*, those hanging flutes of white and pink and coral, rumored to be the favorite of the gods, are closed for the evening. They will re-open ripely to the warming sun next morn. Other exotics like *euphorbia*, *casania*, and *jacaranda* dip and sway in the breeze amid bushes of striped-green leaves shaped like giant elephant ears.

Five silk cushions grace their square, wooden stools. These are placed next to each other in a semi-circle facing an open center. There stands King Farhad greeting his guests with the utmost humility and modesty. Farhad shows Queen Rima to her seat next to his in the center. Princess Yna and General Onor settle to the Queen's left; Counselor Drat'n to His Majesty's right. The King nods and a gong sounds.

Attendants bring forth lacquered trays with sturdy legs and place them before the guests. As musicians strike up evening melodies of gaiety and froth, various delicacies drawn from across the Empire appear on bronze plates or banana leaves. Then an unexpected delight: glass vessels for wine, obtained from the Land of Pyramids and Papyrus. Many toasts ensue and even the stars begin to twinkle with joy. *The repast is going well*, Drat'n observes.

When fruits and dates are served, the Counselor rises to announce: "The world knows of Your Highness's fondness for word-songs." He bows to Queen Rima and her party. "Our Court's Head Scribe will sing one specially composed for this occasion."

He nods and another gong sounds. Rashis the Poet enters.

Rima's heart jumps and her ears burn redly. Never before has she encountered such a beautiful man! At the same time, she instantly distrusts him. *Something about his smile*, she judges sharply. *It is too charming*. She decides to pay him no mind. Yna, on the other hand, cannot take her eyes off Rashis. He seems like an unknown ocean, suddenly washing over her, almost drowning her.

Rashis begins to sing his word-song. He has melted many a candle to create it, knowing what an important service he is performing for his King. His verse pays tribute to the glories and beauties of Vayanak. *A beauty alright*, he watches Queen Rima keenly, *but she is turning away!* Rashis senses instantly that his word-song, though agreeable in meter and rhyme, is ultimately too common. Forced to sing on a subject not of his own choosing, he is a poet not of his own making! Finally, the Poet finishes and the gathering claps politely.

Too politely, Farhad notices. Rashis bows deeply and is about to leave when the King, eager to hold Rima's attention, signals to Rashis to stay. The King turns to the Queen: "Our Scribe's word-song fails to please you, madam."

Rima demurs. "Not at all, brother lord. It was most . . . fine. Our thanks to you and your Scribe." She nods a smile to Rashis, who returns with another deep bow.

"Yet we detect a reserve, madam," Farhad insists, beginning to enjoy this game.

Counselor Drat'n picks up his sovereign's thread and weaves it more diplomatically. "Your Highness is renowned for your word-songs. If we may be so bold, could we invite Queen Rima to honor us with a verse?"

"Yes, Sister," Yna enthuses, not wanting the evening to end, "give us one of your favored word-songs."

And the gathering begins to applaud anew, this time with greater vigor. Rima cannot refuse. *Perhaps now is the occasion to bedazzle the Conqueror*, she thinks.

"Well," Rima concedes, "we cannot disappoint." And she begins to sing of a hummingbird and a bee, each courting a newly opened flower for its sweet nectar within:

"Parched, am I," the bird hums sprightly.
"All I ask is yours most lightly."
"Nay," the bee buzzes shortly,
"Listen not, for the bird's most portly.
He drinks for himself and all day long,
Whereas I make honey for a throng."

The hummingbird and the bee argue thus until a giant wind blows and the flower is dispersed all over the field, leaving both bird and bee bereft of their drink. Undaunted, they fly off to find another flower in another field for another chance at nectar.

The word-song is simple and brief yet it brings a smile to all who hear it. *A most unusual woman,* Farhad appreciates anew.

Everyone applauds happily but something unfelt before stirs within Rashis. He knows not whether it is the purity of the word-song or the beauty of the Queen. He knows only he cannot be bested in his own empire.

"Your Highness." He bows deeply, surprising all with his audacity in addressing the Queen. "Thy word-song humbles with its freshness and grace, brilliance and play. May thy most undeserving servant be permitted to make a second offering to augment my previous lack."

Farhad is about to intervene when Rima, to her own surprise, gestures to the Head Scribe to proceed. Rarely is she challenged and, when she is, she finds her veins pulse a little faster than usual.

Rashis now embarks on one of *his* favored word-songs. No longer restricted to paeans of Vayanak, Rashis turns to a more familiar subject.

"I call it *Love's Final Requite*," he announces. And Rashis begins to sing:

> *Songs of beauty, love, and rapture,*
> *A nightingale sings for all to capture.*
> *Yet never a tune or note sounds in turn,*
> *Under moonlit half-glow or high-noon's burn.*
> *Lonely, the nightingale flies hither and yon*
> *To meet his echo, he hopes, anon.*
> *One morn, as usual, he warbles and trills*
> *To hear – at last! – music that thrills.*
> *A maiden sits by her silk spinning,*
> *While letting flow the sweetest singing.*
> *The nightingale cannot believe his ears!*
> *He has found her, no doubts or worries or fears.*
> *He flies instantly to her side,*
> *With duets a-plenty to confide.*
> *The bird calls out with fervent cheer,*
> *His voice pure, strong, and clear.*
> *Suddenly, he is covered in blindness*
> *Thrown into something not known for kindness.*

Whence he emerges, dismay'd to find
Locked in a cage, forever in bind.
"He'll make a good meal," the man says
*   to the maiden*
She who sits by her sewing a-laden.
"I'll miss his songs," she smiles
*   sadly,*
"But we need to eat so very badly."
The nightingale sings his last,
For his fate is cast.
"I regret nothing, though benighted,
For my love is finally requited."

The gathering sits in silence, then breaks out in enthusiastic applause. Rashis gives a most humble, grateful bow. Outwardly, Rima reveals nothing but her inner being churns with remorse. *This man I thought so shallow and vain actually feels most deeply!*

Farhad sees the Queen is moved, and swells with satisfaction. *She cannot dismiss us as without culture!* he self-congratulates as his tongue expertly tosses out the red spit of a betel nut.

Queen Rima rises and so does the rest of the party. "We thank you, brother lord, for a most entertaining evening. Perhaps we could invite you and your entourage," she nods towards the Poet, "to an excursion next morrow. We have many beautiful waterfalls in Vayanak. 'Twould be a shame for Your Majesty to miss them."

All agree to the Queen's suggestion, relieved not to endure another feast.

Next Morn

To his horror, the Conqueror's belly finally gives way. One evening of delicacies from his own Empire, it seems, has broken its tolerance of five nights of Vayanak's. He cannot make the excursion without undue embarrassment.

"We shall inform the Queen and call off the excursion," Counselor Drat'n recommends solicitously.

"Nay, nay." The Conqueror waves weakly from bed. "You and the rest go. Talk to Onor. It's your only chance."

The Counselor can do little but bow and depart quietly as the Conqueror slips into a fit of snores.

"We cannot proceed without His Majesty," Rima protests upon hearing the news, though her usual, royal bearing limbers slightly. "He lies ill while we frolic in country . . . 'Twould seem uncaring and disrespectful."

"But His Majesty insists," Counselor Drat'n explains.

General Onor steps up. *Better to go*, he thinks, *for there is more than meets the eye here.*

"Perhaps, Your Highness, we should honor our Royal Guest's request. Not to do so would cause unnecessary displeasure."

Rima catches her old mentor's meaning and orders accordingly.

"Very well, General." She signals to Yna to notify the porters, then turns to

Drat'n: "Please extend our regrets and well wishes to your King, along with any medicines and comforts he may need."

And the excursion begins.

The Excursion

Hardy porters carry the Queen and her party, each in a bamboo sedan covered by a brocade canopy on top with curtains of crotched silk on both sides. One blocks the sun; the other welcomes the draft. They form a relatively simple retinue: four porters per dignitary, followed by ten attendants to carry and prepare the noonday meal. The Queen's ladies-in-waiting had begged off the occasion. They could not bear the heat and the exertion, and Rima could not bear to force them.

Down-down-down they descend from the Palace on the mountaintop to the rushing rivers below. Water rolls thunderously over boulders big and small. It encourages some fishes to be quick and lively; others, slow and tranquil.

Wild flowers abound. They wave drunkenly with petals of yellow, pink, purple, and blue amidst a lush greenness that emboldens all. *Truly*, the Counselor inhales deeply, *a garden of dreams*. Drat'n marvels at sights previously unseen: trees whose roots rise to reach their leaves, only to seek ground again, until the tree becomes entwined and thick with its journeys; giant butterflies the size of birds, and birds as small as butterflies, each a riot of color and sound and shape; flowers that beckon with beauty only to display jaws of steel to unsuspecting visitors; tree rodents that soar above with webbed arms; small, furry tribes that walk and peel bananas and cradle babies like people but with long, winding tails; and much much more. Princess Yna brings Caw-Caw who sits quietly and obediently on her shoulder, seemingly awed, too, by Vayanak's wild abundance.

Soon enough, they come upon a royal resting place: a small, open hut. Lake grass thatch above and bamboo stalk walls below, cut squarely in parts for windows. No doors contain the lodging. Erected above the running brook like a bridge on stilts, the doorless hut serves perfectly for the noonday meal.

Attendants unload trays of delectables and spread them on a rush mat over a low-lying table. The Royal Party enters the resting place where large silk cushions await, placed around the setting. Normally, Rashis would join the other attendants outside. But today, he benefits from the Conqueror's absence by taking his place inside.

Hungered by the trip, all partake heartily and the wine flows generously – more for the men than the women. They indulge in stories of fun and laughter, puzzles and puns. Nothing is revealed and yet everything seems open. They appear like any outing of young and old, brothers and sisters, not a royal expedition full of plots and intrigue, strategists and advisors. Somehow, leaving the Palace behind and sharing a simple meal over a musical brook turns royal demands into a faintly irksome memory. Even Caw-Caw dozes peacefully on a perch on the side.

Upon finishing, the Queen and her sister wish to walk a little, a rare freedom. The Counselor and the Poet gallantly offer to escort. General Onor and the others prefer to wait at the hut by the brook. They need their noonday respite.

The foursome strolls forth leisurely and companionably, wrapped in the magic of full bellies and happy conversations while surrounded by the grand benevolence of the gods.

The Queen and the Counselor pace slightly ahead while Yna and Rashis bring up the rear. A revived Caw-Caw surveys all from Yna's shoulder, as is his wont.

"How came you upon word-songs, Sir?" Yna asks, covering her curiosity by feeding Caw-Caw another sunflower seed.

Rashis finds the Princess most charming and unpretentious, despite her high station. *Were she not the Queen's kin . . . Banish the thought!* The Poet looks down, as he strides along with arms folded behind.

"An orphanage took pity on me when I was less than a cycle old," he relates quietly. "My father, a farmer, had died. It was a time of famine and my mother could no longer sustain me. A magistrate who followed the *sutras* had created the orphanage. He convinced local nobles that they could cumulate good credit in this life, to reincarnate well in the next, if they donated monies, food, clothing, and other necessities for orphans. He was *very* persuasive." Rashis smiles charmingly at this recall but Yna can feel the sorrow behind it. "The magistrate was also an accomplished poet," Rashis continues. "And he found in me a willing pupil. I learned much from him. He was like a father to me." Rashis admits this last detail lightly, casually but a touch of gravity still hangs within.

"Why did you leave?" Yna cannot help probing.

Before Rashis can answer, Yna hears Rima calling out to her. A giant, blue-beaked cousin to Caw-Caw is sweeping and swooshing impressively above. Caw-Caw immediately flies off, excited to dance with his kin. Yna drops all else to chase after her errant pet. "Come back, Caw-Caw!" she calls forth angrily yet piteously.

For once in his life, Counselor Drat'n forgets all premeditation. He runs to Yna, waving his arms, hoping to help her catch Caw-Caw's attention and, hopefully, remind the bird of his love of seeds. Eventually, the bird tires of dancing and returns to Yna's shoulder, barking "Seed!" The Counselor and the Princess look at each other, then dissolve into bellyaches of merriment.

Watching the scene, Rima and Rashis find themselves standing closer to each other than Queen and Scribe should. But Rima does not mind. An unexpected sense of belonging fills her, as though they are meant to face the world together. She recognizes him as a mere singer of word-songs but accepts him, also, as much more. *What's the matter with me?* she wonders. At the same time, she treasures the sweetness of the sensation. Rima smiles to herself secretly, delicately. But Rashis catches it. *What beauty and grace!* He cannot repress the urge to address her again, directly.

"Your Highness . . . shall we return?"

Rima looks at the setting sun and reluctantly agrees.

"Ah." She waves to Yna and Drat'n to follow. The Queen and the Poet take the lead back to the doorless hut over the bubbling brook.

"We enjoyed your *Love's Final Requite*," Rima opens shyly. Rashis bows in thanks. "Is it just a song, Head Scribe, or do you truly view love with such a mix of the bitter and the sweet?"

Rashis considers the query.

"I don't know, Your Highness," he answers honestly, lapsing into common speech as though they were peers. "Perhaps, I wish 'tweren't so."

"But is not the sweet possible only because of the bitter, and the bitter tolerable because of the sweet?" Rima queries.

Rashis smiles. "Your Highness is most kind to think so."

"Still, how else could we account for it?" She turns to Rashis inquiringly but the Poet finds himself increasingly lost in those big, dark pools of compassion . . . He catches himself in time to continue with a semblance of mind. He changes tactic.

"Does not serendipity play dangerous tricks, Your Highness? A mighty wind could blow, for instance, leaving a bird and a bee hungry for their flower."

"But they go on, do they not?" Rima smiles. "They know there is always another field with another flower with still more nectar."

"Most reassuring, Your Highness," Rashis now teases, "if one is a bird or a bee."

They share a quiet laugh at the absurdity, like any two young people on the brink of a discovery meant only for them.

By now, they are back at the hut. General Onor, the porters, and the attendants are ready for the long trek back. Ever watchful, the General detects a slight change in the air. The foursome who left for a stroll is not the same who returns now: their faces are flushed from the walk and the open air, with hair and garments slightly wind-blown. The Queen, though, seems removed, while the Princess overly chatty; the Counselor lighter in spirit yet the Poet less so. *Hm*, he notes, withholding judgment for now.

As Rima approaches her sedan, Rashis extends a hand, which she takes, to balance her step. It is a perfectly natural, even expected, act of service from a subject to a Queen. Yet, when their hands touch, a charge like lightning bolts through all who witness it and especially in the two who partake in it.

Rima sinks into her sedan, grateful for the canopy's protection, and not just from the sun.

Drat'n's Accounting

Next morn, as usual, Counselor Drat'n calls upon the Conqueror. Farhad is still in bed but sitting up and downing a bowl of hearty soup. *Something's different*, Farhad attunes straight away as Drat'n enters the King's chamber. Indeed, the Counselor's complexion suffers not from its usual pinched pallor due to late nights reading memorials. And he steps with greater vigor yet with a lightness that exudes from within.

"Happiness becomes you," Farhad comments dryly. "We presume the excursion went well, despite our absence?"

"Sire, we, of course, could not . . ." The Counselor, usually so smooth in speech, stumbles awkwardly.

Farhad waves him quiet. His condition leaves no patience for platitudes. The Conqueror comes directly to the point. "Did you speak to the General, Counselor?"

Drat'n's shoulders clench. He had completely forgotten! In the course of the day, he was so taken by all he had seen and heard and felt, not to mention the walks, the talks, the hilarity with Caw-Caw ... His mission fell aside like a piece of down from a waddling duck! Despite his private, albeit brief, amble with Rima after the noonday meal, he found himself regaling her with his expertise on herbs and medicine, vegetation and cuisine – a consuming side interest – rather than affairs of state. He now perceives how adroitly, how elegantly, the young Queen had inquired about his hobbies, rather than treating him as a Counselor only.

But he cannot report *nothing* to the Conqueror. Drat'n's very life, not to mention his station, depends on it! The Counselor scours his mind for a response.

"Thy humble servant did better than speak to the General, Sire." Drat'n bows obsequiously. "I conversed with Queen Rima herself." The news so surprises Farhad he puts down the soup. Raised brows urge Drat'n to continue. "She inclines favorably towards Your Majesty." *After all*, Drat'n reasons, *we have no evidence to the contrary*.

Farhad presses further: "Does she accept our proposal?"

Drat'n cannot answer otherwise: "Yes, Sire."

Farhad is so pleased, he jumps out of bed calling forth: "Barber! Dresser! I must look my handsomest for my betrothed!"

The Counselor hurries to amend his lie.

"Sire," Drat'n suggests quickly, "perhaps 'twould be best to approach the General first. The subject might be too delicate for the Queen." The Conqueror pauses.

"Indeed, Counselor," he agrees. "Now that the prize is within our grasp, there is no need to offend through haste."

Drat'n breathes a little easier. *I have time to prepare the General, if not the Queen.*

"Allow thy humble servant to meet with the General today to negotiate this matter?" Drat'n asks hopefully.

"Nay," the Conqueror bellows triumphantly, now readying for his barber, "we shall negotiate ourselves!"

Negotiations

"Welcome and greetings, Your Majesty." General Onor bows deeply, along with his full household. They are at the great gate to the General's compound. A messenger has run ahead to announce the Conqueror's arrival. *What's this all about?* the old Regent wonders. "We trust Your Majesty's health is well restored?"

"Yes, yes . . ." Farhad replies perfunctorily. He surveys the General's compound. A goldfish pond sits squarely in the middle. Lovely, large lily pads float within. A few indolent frogs sun themselves on top, occasionally snatching an errant fly with their long, sticky tongues. On both sides of the pond lie two long chambers of teak and bamboo. More chambers line behind these, with still more after them. In all, the General's compound holds three sets of chambers on each side of the goldfish pond. Intricate carvings on each chamber's sliding panels ensure both respite and propriety.

A marble vestibule faces south, connecting the first two sets of chambers. Open in front and back, the vestibule greets honored guests with draft and shade, so conversations could proceed in confidence and comfort, while retaining lightness and light. Leafy, green palms in large clay pots further welcome the guest. Delicate offerings of fruits and nuts await on a small table between two lacquered and spacious seats. *All this will be mine.*

The General escorts the Conqueror to the marble vestibule. They settle in the customary fashion, cross-legged. Onor waits patiently for the Conqueror to open the conversation as an attendant brings two tiny cups of chrysanthemum tea on a tray.

Farhad comes straight to the point: "Her Highness Queen Rima has accepted our proposal."

Though startled, the General reveals not a twitch.

"The Queen has yet to inform her humble servant," Onor responds with half a bow. "I presume Your Majesty received this acceptance directly from Her Highness?"

"Doubt you the veracity of our news?!" the Conqueror demands, incensed that the General would *dare* to suggest anything otherwise.

"Not at all, Your Majesty," General Onor calmly replies. "Please excuse an old man's lack of alacrity. Perhaps Her Highness simply wishes to cherish the news a little longer. It is, after all, of the utmost importance for both Kingdom and Empire, Queen and King."

"Cherish or not," the Conqueror growls, any pretense at etiquette now vanished, "we have waited long enough! Inform the Queen we expect a formal announcement and soon. Our Empire awaits."

The General nods politely.

"Remember," the Conqueror adds menacingly, "our army sits at the bottom of this mountain as your Queen has requested. But my generals call daily. One sign from me and they will come storming."

General Onor bows again in acknowledgment as the Conqueror departs in a blur of indignation.

"He *what*?" Rima grasps her throat. The Queen and her old Regent are in her private chambers.

"King Farhad threatens to overtake the Palace if he does not leave with what he came here for," Onor reports frankly.

Rima sinks onto her bed.

"But our assent was never given. How came he to this assertion?"

"Perhaps the Conqueror is forcing a decision by staking this claim," the old Regent deciphers.

The Queen turns to her old mentor. "What say you, General?"

He regards her kindly but firmly. "Accept him, Your Highness. There is no other choice. The Conqueror may resort to unseemly measures but we are no match for his army." Unexpectedly, Rima looks away and panic begins to seize the General. "Highness, you cannot think otherwise!" He sees in his mind what he hopes never to see again: burnings and lootings, killings and rapes, tortures and enslavements. And the screaming – of men, women, and children, running in desperation to every-where and nowhere all at once. *Nay*, he vows, *it cannot happen again!*

"I – We . . . cannot," Rima confesses almost in a whisper, looking down.

"Why not, Child?" General Onor forgets all royal protocol and resumes his old form of address for her.

"Onor-pa," she returns the courtesy, speaking in the voice of childhood intimacy, "he has revealed himself as mostly Conqueror and little man. No word-songs can withstand such iron will. How can we sustain ourselves – and Vayanak – under these conditions?"

"We have no choice, Child." The General knows his ruse has failed. Of course no word-song would affect a man like Farhad but the General had hoped to soften Rima's disposition in the meanwhile. *Does she not see what will happen if she refuses?* Suddenly, the General recalls the doorless hut over the bubbling brook and the foursome who returned from their stroll – and the hands that touched. "Is there something – or someone – that obstructs your acceptance of the King?"

"Of course not!" Rima protests but the red blotches, swarming her neck, give her away.

"This is no time for sentiment, Child! He is but a singer of word-songs! Should the Conqueror get wind of this, he will spare neither Poet nor Queen!"

Rima rises stiffly and addresses her former Regent formally: "We will decide, General Onor, according to *our* will." She holds up a hand as Onor attempts to intervene. "Rest assured, we will not – we would *never* – jeopardize the welfare of our Kingdom and our people under any circumstance."

"What shall I tell His Majesty?" the old Regent asks, suddenly feeling his age doubled. A dull ache begins to throb behind one eye.

"Tell him . . ." Rima answers slowly, "we shall declare our decision on the day of the next full moon."

"That is more than a fortnight away." The General leans slightly on a side table for support. "Will the Conqueror wait that long?"

"He will," Rima replies. "Tell him, in Vayanak, the morn of a full-moon day signifies the most auspicious time for a royal announcement of the magnitude he expects."

The General has little choice but to bow in compliance to his Queen.

Meanwhile, the Conqueror has returned to his quarters, impatiently dispensing with the bothersome fineries he had donned to meet with the General.

"Drat'n!" he commands.

The Counselor appears seemingly out of nowhere.

"At your service, Sire." He bows deeply.

"The old man knows nothing of the Queen's acceptance!" King Farhad thunders. "Yet he is her closest advisor. How goes it?!"

Drat'n has an answer well prepared. "Perhaps," the Counselor suggests, "Her Highness speaks well to one but ill to another and still nothing to a third."

"To what end?" the Conqueror demands.

"Queen Rima is sovereign, after all, of a Kingdom with great cultural refinements but little military capability. She must resort to artifice and lies, manipulations and deceits. Such are the weapons of the weak."

"What is your recommendation, then?" the Conqueror glowers at his Counselor.

Drat'n leans in with a lowered voice. "We do the same."

The Conqueror roars back in laughter.

"The war, it begins."

Message and Messenger

Rashis waits anxiously inside the doorless hut over the bubbling brook. A single, small candle keeps him company. In the dark of night, the brook seems to gurgle loudly, almost overwhelmingly. *Or is it my heart?* he wonders. *Who would have thought this possible?*

Rashis re-reads the banana leaf gripped in his hand: "*Nary a moment passes, without tender reminisces/The doorless hut, the musical brook/Even a Queen sends it flying kisses.*" A drawn half-moon ends the missive, indicating to meet tonight.

This must come from Rima, Rashis the Lover wishes fervently. *Who else could it be?* And yet, Rashis the Poet cannot help but wonder why the word-song is slightly clumsy, off-meter. It does not resemble Rima's usual, careful compositions. *Perhaps the note was written in haste*, Rashis convinces himself.

A crackle interrupts these thoughts. He turns to the front of the hut. Hurried foot-steps crumble the pebbles that line its walkway. A woman's lone figure approaches, shadowy in floating chiffon. His heart stops.

"The gods be thanked you are here," she whispers while lifting her veil.

Rashis falls back a step, so surprised, is he, to find Yna standing before him.

"I know," Yna allows in common speech, "you were expecting someone else."

Rashis catches his breath and realizes the situation. The hand that gripped the banana leaf with such eagerness now crushes it in disappointment.

"I knew 'twas too good to be true!" he lets out bitterly.

"Nay," Yna draws closer to Rashis, fearing their voices would carry. "The Queen cares for you deeply. But our lives are not ours to determine. She has her duty just as you have yours. You must know your sentiments place you in grave danger. For this reason, she sent me to beg you to leave. Flee before it's too late!" Yna takes from her robe a small cloth bag tied at the ends with cotton yarn and bulging with precious stones. "Take this." She thrusts the bag in front of the poet. "It will take you far."

But Rashis turns away, running a hand through thick, black curls.

"Flee where?" he laughs mournfully. "To whom?"

"Have you nowhere to go? No one to harbor you?" Yna reaches out in sympathy, barely touching his shoulder. Strangely, her breath cuts short and quickens.

Rashis returns Yna's gentle urging with anger and remorse and pain: "You once asked why I left the magistrate who was like a father to me. I'll tell you why: he threw me out! His most favored daughter, the one as talented in word-song as he, had fallen in love with me, and I with her . . .! Though just beyond childhood, we were old enough to marry. But he could not have a nobody-orphan as a son-in-law. His illustrious ancestors would not tolerate it! Soon enough, a suitable match was found in a nobleman from another county. The night before she left, I begged her to run away with me. But she had not the courage. Tears were her only recourse. And I found myself a vagrant, a vagabond – until His Majesty's Counselor heard me trade word-songs at a road-side inn for a few, measly morsels."

"We are not like your magistrate, my sister and I," Yna responds quietly. "We know the whims of the gods can be cruel. We stand by those we love."

"These are fine words, young one," Rashis charges in the candle's half-glow, his visage heart-breakingly handsome despite the contempt in his voice. "But what of action?"

Yna lowers her gaze. Only silence follows.

"Nay," the Poet dismisses the Princess, "you nobles are all alike."

But Yna replies to Rashis with an unforeseen maturity and resolve. "I mean what I say, Sir. And I dare to act on what I say."

An impulse floods the Poet. He cares not for the consequences.

"Dare you act on your words for me?" He stands close to her, challenging her.

"For you but, most of all, for me," she returns forthrightly. And she comes to him, as he takes her, in the black pitch of night, under a half-moon drowned in the roiling rhythms of the gurgling brook.

Discoveries

The full moon's eve arrives. Vayanak's Court readies for the Queen's announcement next morn. Many whisper "nuptials," as a steady stream of caravans, bearing different peoples and goods, arrive onto the Palace grounds. *A feast in the making*, they suppose.

Queen Rima and General Onor are conferring in her antechamber. Yna sits nearby stroking Caw-Caw. *She seems quiet of late.* Rima looks at her sister at one point. *Perhaps she was too young for her mission?* Rashis refuses to leave, Yna reported. He feels it unmanning. Rima sighs inwardly. Affairs of state – they are unrelenting at times.

Suddenly, they receive word that the Conqueror is in the Council Hall. He requests a word with Her Highness. *At this hour of night?* all three wonder. But no one voices it. Each hurries to the Hall.

"To what do we owe this pleasure, brother lord?" Rima addresses Farhad formally yet with a touch of imperiousness. "Are we not seeing Your Majesty in this very Hall early next morn?"

The Conqueror bows elaborately to the Queen.

"'Tis so, madam," Farhad slurs.

He is drunk! Rima signals an attendant to seat His Majesty. His uncertain footing threatens both his person and the marble floor. The attendant orders two sub-attendants to haul forth the Hall's most imposing armchair, made of mahogany and ivory.

"Our ardor for Your Highness –" the Conqueror slumps carelessly into the chair "– cannot wait."

Counselor Drat'n steps forward to explain. "His Majesty would like an assurance before the assembly next morn."

"Assurance?" Rima repeats the word incredulously. *What is going on?*

The Conqueror twirls his finger to his Counselor to continue. Drat'n withdraws from his robe a crumpled banana leaf.

"We have on good authority, Your Highness –" he waves the banana leaf in the air "– of improper relations between a member of your royal household and a member of ours." He hands the banana leaf to an attendant who serves it to the Queen.

General Onor and Princess Yna stand by mutely: one in shock; the other, despair.

"Surely, Counselor –" Rima throws the banana leaf disdainfully on the floor "– you cannot insinuate anything from this. Anyone could have sent this message. What links it to our household?"

"This was found at the trysting site." The Counselor pulls another item from inside his robe. This time: a silk handkerchief with Vayanak's royal seal embroidered on it. Only Queen Rima and Princess Yna have use of this seal.

"Again," Rima derides, "a thief could do as well!"

"I had hoped," Drat'n regrets, "to avoid this." The Counselor now offers his final evidence: a handful of seeds. Yna alone carries these seeds to feed Caw-Caw. And everyone knows she carries them in a pouch inside her gown. The seeds would fall out only if her garment, similarly, falls off.

But Rima remains defiant. "These are but *things* you throw before us," the Queen counters her accuser. "You have no proof in person."

Counselor Drat'n nods to a guard who leads out Rashis the Poet. Rima had hoped he'd be ragged and torn, his testimony a ripped confession. Instead, the Poet appears untouched, handsome and fit as ever. Rima regrets to her marrow she ever held feelings for this man.

"Need we say more, Your Highness?" Counselor Drat'n appeals archly.

The Queen's visage turns translucent. Rima now awakens to the damage done to her triply. Sovereign, lover, sister – all have betrayed her trust. Farhad is to be expected but Rashis . . . and, most painfully, Yna? *Fool and fools!* Yet she cannot reveal any inner turmoil – especially in front of a drunken brute like the Conqueror. Seemingly absent-mindedly, Rima re-arranges the folds of her silk shawl. The redness blotching her neck no longer shows. She faces the Counselor calmly and speaks with a quiet, deadly reserve. "What is your demand?"

The Counselor bows unctuously. "Should Your Highness decide in favor of entering into wedded bliss with His Majesty King Farhad," Drat'n unfolds the deal, "then, of course, all will be forgotten. But, should Your Highness decide otherwise, we will be forced to expose the person who has defiled your Kingdom and your Royal House. 'Twill be difficult, then, for Vayanak to continue its glorious legacy as the gem of culture in the known world."

Filthy men! Rima feels like spitting. *They can whore and rape and commit all sorts of foul deeds yet the world still crowns them titles like "The Great" or "The Magnificent." But when a woman, especially a young one, makes a single misstep, she and all around her are condemned to eternity.* Rima looks not at her sister. She knows Yna must be trembling with fear and shame. Queen Rima rises and turns to King Farhad still slumped in his chair.

"Your Majesty will not be disappointed in the morrow. I bid you a good night!" With that, Rima leaves the Hall.

Normally, sister and Regent would have followed their Queen but, this evening, they are rooted in place as if petrified.

King Farhad and his Counselor grin at each other smugly. *Success!* Everything is proceeding as planned. Once married, Farhad can return to empire-building, expanding his territory, his name, and his rule! And serving under him will be the ever resourceful Drat'n, no matter how pale his pallor or how stained his fingers from reading memorials late into night. As for the Queen of Vayanak – she will be their most eminent hostage. *Women*, Farhad chuckles to himself, *they are so easy!* He entertains a moment of nostalgia. *How I long for the days of worthy adversaries. Warriors! Heroes! Conquerors. That is,* he concludes, *men like ourself.*

Only Rashis cannot raise his eyes to meet anyone's, especially Yna's.

The Announcement

Next morn arrives, a brilliant blue of a day. Vayanak's full Court is assembled in the Council Hall. Heading the gathering is His Majesty King Farhad. He is seated in the same mahogany-and-ivory armchair he slumped in the night before. Unusually, Farhad exudes good cheer. *Let her take her time*, he bides patiently. *The farce will soon end.* Behind his sovereign is Counselor Drat'n. He bears his prominence with extreme humility, knowing his position will become even more important after this day. At the far end of the assembly, near the royal podium, stands Rashis the Poet. As a member of His Majesty's retinue, he must be present. But he holds himself apart, eyes downcast, as if attending a funeral.

Finally, the brass bells ring. The Court bows in greeting to their Queen.

Rima enters, a vision in silk the color of hibiscus in Summer. General Onor and Princess Yna follow. Though each appears as expected, both seem unduly somber. Princess Yna looks as though sleep had evaded her all night. *Must be all the excitement*, onlookers gabble.

Rima reaches the Throne and turns to her Court as well as King Farhad: "Good people of Vayanak — and Your Majesty King Farhad — we salute you."

Farhad gallantly half-bows from his chair.

The Queen continues: "Today, we have a momentous decision to announce — a decision that will need your utmost support.

"As you all know, His Majesty King Farhad has graced Vayanak with a proposal to join our two Kingdoms through matrimony. We are most honored by this invitation to union and have given it much consideration. His Majesty is a great Warrior and Conqueror, a Sovereign of Seven Realms, a King in all ways —" Farhad smiles benevolently to one and all as the Queen sings his praises "— but one."

He sits up. *What?*

"Of Warrior and Conqueror, Sovereign and King," he hears the Queen say, "little else remains. Should we join our Kingdoms,

Vayanak would benefit His Majesty with its culture and refinements, extending his legacy beyond territory and time, but our Kingdom would disappear as simply another piece of conquest. We would lose our laws and customs, our arts and philosophies, our way of being for . . . what? And we will have given Vayanak to the Conqueror on a platter piled high with the wailings and lamentations of our Ancestors!"

Counselor Drat'n looks around nervously. Both Onor and Yna are struck dumb. But the rest of the Court is murmuring in agreement, increasingly agitated by this stranger, this interloper, this ruinous thief!

Farhad kicks back his chair. It lands loudly, cracking the marble floor and silencing the assembly.

"How *dare* you refuse me!" he snarls, demonstrating in person what Rima has just described in words. "My army will crush you!"

"We think not," Rima replies evenly. She nods and more than one hundred strapping young men and women, ranging in age from less than one to more than two cycles, step from a curtain at the end of the Hall. Each wears a warrior's leather straps, even the women, and holds a bow with arrows or a full-length spear. Farhad turns around in disbelief.

"Who . . .?" he croaks.

"May we introduce to Your Majesty, your sons and daughters." Rima sweeps her hand graciously to include all the surprise guests.

General Onor, the Queen's mentor and former Regent, cannot believe the scene before him. *How . . .? When . . .? Why didn't she tell me?*

The Queen continues: "These are the souls you sired but discarded as scraps the moment your army found another war to fight, another territory to conquer."

Farhad turns to his Counselor but Drat'n's wits have abandoned him long ago. The Conqueror suddenly laughs long and hard.

"Welcome, imperial progeny!" He holds out his arms. Farhad faces Rima: "Our thanks for this family reunion. They are, after all, the fruits of our royal loins. They will do as *we* command!"

Rima returns with a smile. "Forgive us, brother lord." The Queen nods again. "We failed to introduce their mothers."

Attendants draw open the curtains behind the Queen and four dozen women now step in front. They also range in age: a few look barely out of childhood with infants in their arms; others seem like their mothers and grandmothers. But each stares at the Conqueror stonily. Rima can only imagine what they must be feeling, finally face-to-face with their rapist and on equal terms. *Justice must bend the pain*, she surmises.

Farhad's laughing face freezes in place. Counselor Drat'n's remains stupefied. Rashis cannot believe what is unfolding before him. Neither can the rest of the Court. Never has such an event happened before, from mythical to present times!

"These mothers," Rima informs the Conqueror, "have raised their children well. Seared into their memories is how you took women on whim and left them at will, never bothering even to learn their names. They have had to fare for themselves, in poverty and isolation, after fathers and uncles, brothers and cousins cast them out, especially with the children who reminded them daily of the women's shame and defilement, and the men's impotence and ineptitude. Households cried rivers of tears but did nothing. Yet these women never abandoned their babes. Steeled by misfortune and girded by the gods, they cared for the innocents that issued from their wombs, no matter the circumstance, and brought them up to love and respect what is truly beautiful and pure. These sons and daughters, brother lord, would do anything for their mothers – even if it means defeating their father. Along the way, mothers and children, sisters and brothers, have amassed armies of their own, composed of those who, like them, have been conquered and used and thrown away by you."

"Our imperial forces outnumber any ragtag band of bandits!" the Conqueror shouts, though cringing a little despite his awesome power.

"'Tis true," Rima responds, "but each of your soldiers, every one of your generals, has a mother. They may rape and pillage as warriors but they cannot withstand a mother's stern eye. Once faced by these women who could be their mothers or grandmothers – and the younger ones, their daughters or wives – your army will dissolve in dispute and disarray." Rima looks Farhad straight in the eyes. "Power, brother lord, comes not only from the blade of a sword or the pierce of an arrow. These are but temporary instruments of conquest. There is another kind of power that lasts beyond one conquest or even many, one lifetime or several, but which you have sneered at as weak or useless or womanly; it comes from that forging of sentiment when a newborn babe suckles at its mother's breast, hearing the songs that coo it to sleep, and basking in the devotion that tenders it into youth and maturity. Your inattention to love, brother lord, will sustain *our* Throne but cost you yours. Such is the wisdom of culture."

"Witch!" the Conqueror sputters from foaming, purple lips. His fingers twitch, as is his habit, whenever engorged by rage. A familiar sight to Rashis, the Poet, who flies out in front just as Farhad flings his silver dagger, always tucked in his belt, toward the Queen. The dagger hits with a lethal thud. And Rashis falls to the floor, clutching his heart.

The Court screams and scuffles. Vayanak's royal guards immediately surround Queen Rima and General Onor to protect them from further assaults. The One Hundred likewise cage their father and Counselor Drat'n with pointed weapons, holding both hostage.

Yna rushes to Rashis's side, lifting his head to her lap, to keep the blood spilling from his mouth from choking his throat.

"Forgive . . ." Rashis attempts.

"Nay, nay," Yna soothes. Crystal tears drop onto his red, raw wound as if to heal it.

Rashis tries a gallant smile but fails. He taps a finger feebly on the bloody swamp that is now his chest. Yna pulls from his robe a folded banana leaf, and the Poet closes his eyes. Yna cradles the corpse tightly and vows in a whisper, "You will live in me forever!"

Aftermath

King Farhad is arrested but held at General Onor's compound rather than the guest quarters. Lock and key detain Counselor Drat'n elsewhere. Onor aims to keep Farhad's generals in ignorance for as long as possible. All members of the Court, including the One Hundred and their mothers, have sworn an oath of silence. Onor pays homage again to Vayanak's ancestors for building a Palace so high in the sky.

The General will deal with Farhad soon enough. But his old ailment strikes again, as pain pierces through his eye. *Not now, of all times!*

Rima enters Yna's bedchamber. It resembles the Queen's in all respects, only smaller. Caw-Caw sits on his perch in the corner, nibbling the wood. Sensitive to his mistress, the bird remains unusually quiet. Rima sees Yna standing by an open, arched window. It overlooks a thistle of roses blooming amid magnolia trees. But the Princess sees them not today. Tears flow as Yna reads a banana leaf drenched in blood, now drying.

"Yna," Rima commands. "You owe me an explanation as your sister and as your Queen!"

Yna turns around and quickly curtsies while wiping her eyes with a silk handkerchief – the kind Drat'n used as evidence of her tryst with Rashis.

"Please forgive me, Sister." Yna cannot help but break into new sobs as she utters these words. She falls to Rima's feet and the older one's heart relents. She bends down and embraces the younger one.

In a softer tone, Rima urges: "Tell me what happened, Bina."

"I tried as you had instructed, Sister, but somehow, he . . . I . . ." She cannot finish.

Rima hugs her sister, understanding all too well what happened. *Would I have acted any differently?* Rima wonders and has to conclude, *Nay*. She leads Yna to the cushioned bench under the window. The two can now speak more comfortably and freely.

"He left this." Yna shoves into Rima's hands the banana leaf from Rashis. It bears a few, simple lines:

> "Bitter is my cup but I had to drink from it.
>
> Last half-moon, the Conqueror told me he had found my mother, now old and frail. He promised to care for her 'til the end of her days – if I would do his bidding.
>
> If not . . . I could not refuse!
>
> Forgiveness, I dare not ask, but perhaps understanding.
>
> I am condemned yet content. Unlike the bird and the bee, I seek no other. I have found my final requite. It is enough to last twenty lifetimes."

Both Rima and Yna suspect the Poet intended to end his life after delivering the letter. But only Rima understands the meaning of the bird and the bee seeking "no other." Rashis meant these words for her. She remembers vividly their exchange during that walk in the wilds of Vayanak.

* * *

"But they go on, do they not?" Rima said of the hummingbird and the bee in her word-song. "They know there is always another field with another flower with still more nectar."

"Most reassuring, Your Highness," Rashis had teased, "if one is a bird or a bee."

* * *

Rashis's letter, then, is addressed to both of them. And Rima finds a small measure of comfort in that.

"You know, Bina," she tells her sister whose sobs have quieted somewhat, "it was a trap. That's why I sent you to warn him."

"How did you know, Sister?" Yna's eyes widen even as they are soaked in tears.

"I received this." Rima pulls from her sleeve another banana leaf, also written in word-song, this time pretending in Rashis's voice to tryst with the Queen at the doorless hut by the gurgling brook on that half-moon night. Rima points to the tell-tale signs of its inauthenticity: yellow stains from black-tea ashes. "Only Counselor Drat'n could have made these," Rima affirms. "I knew it the moment I saw these marks of his office. He must have written in haste, else he would not have left a record of his treachery."

"What about the word-song to Rashis? The one Counselor Drat'n used to demand their 'assurance'?"

"Drat'n wrote that one, also, for I certainly did not." Rima holds her sister by the shoulders and looks her in the eye.

"Farhad schemed all along to use Rashis to seduce us – he knew we were innocents! – so the brute could maneuver an outcome rather than rely on the vagaries of fortune." Rima's complexion turns translucent. "Sending both word-songs, each enticing the other to meet, must mean they did not trust Rashis to enter into their scheme. They could only pressure him to take advantage if he thought 'twas I who sought the tryst." Rima pauses. "This must mean, Bina, that Rashis was an honorable man, in the end. He may have succumbed to the moment but I have no doubt, he was also moved by your kindness toward him and your sweet, pure beauty."

Yna turns to Rima, tears streaming down anew.

"You forgive me, Sister, even though I have shamed you and defied you?"

Rima embraces Yna as in times of old.

"Nothing could lessen my love for you, Bina," Rima avows. "You are heart of my heart, soul of my soul, now and forever. I would never forsake you." And the two sisters abandon themselves to a well-earned cry.

A Bowl of Soup

General Onor has the prisoner, King Farhad, brought to his special greeting room. The ache in the old Regent's eye pounds mercilessly. He needs, more than ever, the room's dark, soothing shade. *A fitting place*, the General notes wryly, *for a man of dark deeds*.

"Unshackle him," the General orders.

The Conqueror gratefully rubs his sore wrists and ankles.

"About time, Onor," Farhad speaks with more brio than expected. "How long are we to play this game?"

"'Tis long enough," Onor agrees. He rings a bell and an attendant brings his favored almond soup, always prepared whenever the General enters this room. "Bring another bowl," Onor instructs. "We cannot overlook our Royal Guest here. But make it empty. I've not enough appetite today."

Farhad settles himself comfortably into the spacious seat across from Onor. *I knew he'd come around! Let's now conclude matters as only men can.*

The attendant brings a second porcelain bowl with matching spoon. Onor pours half of his soup into it, and hands the new bowl to Farhad. The Conqueror eyes it suspiciously at first. But, since Onor begins to drink his, Farhad feels safe to do the same. He, too, likes sweet almond soup.

"Our deal —" Farhad slurps a big mouthful "— was that you would deliver the Queen to us. You were the one who informed us of the Poet's seductions, though you probably never suspected we would use it to seek an 'assurance', eh? You thought, at most, we would rid the Poet one way or another. But Counselor Drat'n is too clever for that! And Rashis, that devil! He was told to bait the Queen but, when she failed to bite, he bagged the sister, instead! Inventive fellow . . . Though true to form, the Poet would not comply without some additional inducements." Farhad smarms on, oblivious to the General's stoic silence. In the midst of crowing, the Conqueror suddenly stops short: "What happened with the One Hundred and their mothers? Had you knowledge of this?"

"The Queen did not share with me this stratagem," the General answers simply. "She must have feared I would object. After all, where's the power in women?"

Farhad grunts in agreement, too busy is he downing the soup.

"I presume we must overthrow her now." Farhad holds the bowl over his lips to catch every last drop. His belly could not take enough of the soothing almond soup after all the turmoil it has suffered!

"Nay," the General replies.

The Conqueror drops his bowl. It cracks not on the polished teak floor but rolls emptily and comically until flipping over.

Onor continues: "I betrayed my Queen to save her, not to destroy her. I could not abide another war and against an army far superior to ours. Only disaster could result! My hope was that she would forget the Poet once he was gone and accept her duty to wed you. But I was too caught in old ways. I could not perceive what she did."

The General slaps his knee with delight. "She was able to defeat you without fighting you! The student has surpassed the teacher. But you! You are a sore that keeps on festering. So I must destroy you now to save her later."

The Conqueror stares mutely. Grabbing his throat, he falls down flat, convulsing. Within moments, all motions cease and his limbs stiffen.

General Onor observes the Conqueror's demise from his rattan couch. When the Conqueror is no more, the old Regent finishes his share of the almond soup, and arranges himself comfortably on the couch. Soon enough, he, too, passes on to the next world, knowing his confession is already in the hands of the Queen.

Three Moons On

Rima sits in the garden of roses and magnolia. She still cannot believe the lightning events of the past three moons.

Her old mentor is now gone. Though he perpetrated a fourth betrayal, she cannot exile him from her memory or her heart. 'Twas he who made her into the Queen she is today! Rima's royal bearing caves a little. Too often of late, she has felt the weight of all the world on her one person. The Queen must decide all! Yet she has no one to lean on or confide in when tired or discouraged, not even a sister.

$\star$ $\star$ $\star$

"You know you must leave," Rima gently told Yna with all the resolve she could muster. "The Court will treat you harshly, even though you are the Queen's kin." Rima held her sister's hand. "You will go with all the provisions I can send. As long as I live and sit on this Throne — and even long afterwards! — you will not want for anything."

Yna nodded quiescently.

"I will care for his mother and his child." She rubbed her growing belly. "They are my destiny now. We will go to the Grand Mystic Peaks where no one knows us. O Sister, will we ever see each other again?"

"If not in this lifetime, Bina, then in the next and twenty lifetimes! Never forget, our fates are entwined."

And the two sisters bade each other a heartrending farewell.

The Queen's parting from Counselor Drat'n fared more lightly. She conveyed the news to him that his sovereign, King Farhad, was no more — a victim of poison that also killed the poisoner. Drat'n immediately begged for admission into Queen Rima's employ.

"How could you contemplate such a possibility when you, in your former role, attempted to entrap us in order to dethrone us?" Rima asked incredulously.

"I may be many things, Your Highness," Drat'n supplicated, "but stupid is not one of them. I made sure to affix those yellow stains on the tryst letter. I knew Your Highness would recognize them since you are, after all, a sovereign used to reading memorials."

Rima had to smile at such honest duplicity.

"And why would you defy your sovereign by exposing your treachery?" Rima had to know.

"'Twas a gamble, to be sure," the Counselor could not resist expounding on his genius. "Should Your Highness discover the origin of the letter, then the Conqueror would have been defeated and Your Highness triumphed. But should Your Highness miss this detail, then the Conqueror would have triumphed and Your Highness defeated. Either way, I would have benefited from my service." Drat'n bows deeply. "But I must convey, Your Highness," the Counselor adds, "my utmost happiness for the former rather than the latter."

"Certainly, Counselor," Rima concurred, "stupid you are not. But neither are you loyal nor sincere nor wise. For all these lacks, our Court cannot abide you. Though fear not, you will always find employ with one master or another. Indeed, you may serve many masters over many lifetimes until you honor your talents rather than sell them like a beggar on the streets."

The Counselor could not fathom the Queen's meaning, despite all his genius. *More female hogwash*, he dismissed.

★ ★ ★

Yet Rima's forecast bears well. Farhad's most powerful general, now with conquering visions of his own (avenging Farhad's death not one of them), took in Drat'n as his Counselor. They battle today with the One Hundred over Farhad's territories.

Vayanak remains untouched. The Council of Mothers had vowed never to embroil Vayanak in their wars. Or, if war does break out, their forces would protect Vayanak with all their might. After all, the Mothers agreed, they owe their present prominence to Queen Rima. Without support from a state power, the Council of Mothers would have remained a band of bandits, forever roaming the world for providence. For this reason, they secretly contacted Queen Rima the moment they heard of Farhad's plan to betroth her. They figured, and rightly, that no reigning Queen would agree to marry Farhad – especially if the Council of Mothers could offer a better alternative. Their only condition: the Queen can confide in no one, neither sister nor former Regent. The risks were too great. In turn, they acceded to Rima's request that Vayanak continue to supply all parties with much-needed goods and supplies, given its circulations of the sea.

Three moons on and the Kingdom flourishes, Rima is gratified to note.

"Your Highness," a young handmaiden interrupts Rima's thoughts. She is the latest member of the royal household. "Please forgive the intrusion but the Council of Mothers is awaiting."

Rima smiles. In many ways, the handmaiden reminds her of Yna. The handmaiden, in turn, cannot thank the gods enough for her good fortune. *What a Queen!* she adulates. *What a woman.*

Rima squares her bearing and lifts her head. Every three moons she meets with the Council of Mothers to confer about order in the world. Plenty of rapists mask as sovereigns and must be stopped. Yet Rima cannot stem the irony of her thoughts today.

I lead the Council of Mothers when I, alone, am not a mother and never will be one. For what king or lord would dare marry me now? Nor am I inclined to marry. How can I forfeit my standing to any man? 'Til date, I am the most powerful Queen in the known world. Yet I am also bereft of all who love me and whom I love.

Suddenly, a never-before thought enters her mind: *What if I were not born a Queen? Might I have a happier, less burdensome life?* But she shakes the notion away. *Too much to do, too many need us, too little time.*

"Your Highness . . .?" the little hand-maiden nudges gently.

"We are coming," Rima replies and walks purposefully into the Palace.

Mythic Recalibrations

The Five Mythic Ones pause in their viewing of the game. It had not turned out as expected.

True, each pair could claim victory. Power and Wealth are needed for happiness in the world, as demonstrated by the Council of Mothers and their alliance with Vayanak. Similarly, Queen Rima and Princess Yna, as embodiments of Power and Wealth, have a tie that cannot tear no matter how much some may try. Human happiness also cannot do without Love and Security. Why else would Rashis the Poet and Onor the General willingly sacrifice their lives? Lastly, Knowledge unlocks Power and Wealth, Love and Security for nothing can happen without it.

"But even if you win . . ." the Laughing Monk reminds the Mythic Ones.

"We lose," the Metallic One commiserates.

For, it is also apparent to all, that simply pairing Power with Wealth or Love with Security or valuing Knowledge is not enough. What matters is *how*.

"*Power more is power less*," the Fiery One of Power recalls the first line of the Laughing Monk's bet. Indeed, Queen Rima has more power than ever but she is also more alone than ever. As for the Conqueror, he dies an ignoble death.

"*Wealth finds not in what's possess'd*," the Metallic One of Wealth echoes in turn. Princess Yna forgoes all *things*, even as a kingdom's Treasurer, to protect the richness of life that lives in her and through her but that she could never possess.

"*Security seeks strength but quakes, instead,*" the Earthy One of Security laments. General Onor desires security so much he comes to fear it, thereby jeopardizing it all the more!

"*Love fans all except the head.*" The Arboreal One of Love cannot stop weeping, its sap threatening to flood all around it. Rashis the Poet only feels love, never *thinking* about it; hence, he played at love only to be played by love.

"*And knowledge knows much but realizes little,*" rounds out the Watery One of Knowledge, "*forever missing the sacred middle!*" Counselor Drat'n has the opposite problem: he only thinks and rarely feels, thereby always serving masters and never mastering himself.

The Mythic Ones consider these realizations in silence, each sunk in the story of their human selves. Soon enough, they argue and shout, point and stomp.

"One throw is not enough!" they demand. "Let us play again with different players at different times under different conditions."

The Laughing Monk congenially agrees. But after twenty throws of twenty lifetimes, each turns out with similar betrayals and violence, conquest and rape, loneliness and exile, shame and disappointment – until

Sihar and Shenya. They make a small break, finally, from the usual pattern. Together, they indicate the possibility of something different, something new.

Instead of setting aggrieved mothers to rectify brutal fathers or upsetting military power with cultural power, always existing in a state of struggle or unrest, Sihar and Shenya show the beauty of balance. It comes from them in relation to each other as well as with their world. Hence, Nature can advise Kings. Wars need not take place. Nobles and farmers, men and women can find common ground, even as each stays distinctively different, without one having to surrender to the other. People can realize their inner dreams simply by sharing them. And brothers and sisters can co-rule.

Such balance comes not easily. To attain it, Sihar and Shenya had to endure harsh tests of love and compassion, honor and commitment, friendship and loyalty, joy and happiness. And these tests cut across Time. Debts to all those transgressed against in the past, even in another lifetime, must be paid, for these account for the present *and* the future.

The Mythic Ones ponder their game. Knowledge is the first to address the Laughing Monk.

"We have learned much from these throws," the Watery One thanks the Laughing Monk. "Perhaps this is the beginning of wisdom?"

"Or another kind of love?" the Arboreal One adds hopefully.

"Or of Power?" "Security?" "Wealth?" The Fiery One, the Earthy One, and the Metallic One each interjects in turn.

"Maybe all of them, or maybe none at all!" The Laughing Monk chuckles merrily. "Who knows?"

"I see," the Watery One murmurs. "It all depends."

"Depends on what?" the Earthy One persists, not quite catching this abstract talk.

"On who, what, when, where, how, and why!" the Arboreal One pipes up.

"How do *you* know?" the Fiery One challenges.

"That's what Love is all about!" the Arboreal One returns happily. "How else can it take place?"

Now the Watery One knows why it's always drawn to Love. What comes instinctively to Love has taken scholars millennia to discover. They may paean Love, debate it, and even enjoy it in their own lives, but rarely do they recognize Love as a kind of Knowledge. Love is always seen as too removed from Knowledge to count. But, really, they are intimately related. A second insight suddenly ripples through the Watery One: they are *all* related! Power, Wealth, Love, Security, Knowledge. Each one needs the others not just to make sense of the Universe but, also, simply to *be*.

The Watery One sinks deeply into these thoughts, leaving the rest of the Mythic Ones in an awkward silence. It takes the Metallic One to pose the final, practical question to the Laughing Monk.

"What if we were to concede a loss *this* time, what is your demand?"

The Laughing Monk regards the Mythic Ones with mirthful eyes and points to the figures of Sihar and Shenya, sitting under the Ancient One by the bubbling brook, facing the evening of their lives.

"Let them have another thirty years," the monk proposes. "They deserve it – unless, of course –" he winks "– something comes up."

"Who knows?" the Watery One copies the Laughing Monk.

"Indeed," the monk concurs, "one or both of them may be called to attend elsewhere. The world needs more Sihars and Shenyas."

The Watery One had not considered this possibility. It turns deeply blue.

"Fair enough!" The others gratefully seal the deal, relieved the payment is so easy. And they celebrate the end of this round of the game with an immense feast, eating and drinking, teasing and joking, sometimes breaking into song, and, of course, laughing heartily along with the Laughing Monk.

★ ★ ★

And so we leave Sihar and Shenya, Gentle Friend, chatting quietly away. It is remarkably unremarkable, you say? That is the secret and the magic! Glad you see it.

Alas I, too, must now bid farewell. Where am I going? I'll find out once I get there! Really, Gentle Friend, your queries induce the greatest bursts of joy from me.

Now where is my walking stick? Ah, here it is! And my trusty bowl? I know, it's slightly chipped along the edge, but never mind! I'm on my way.

Many thanks for listening to my stories. May you live a life as full of love and meaning and unremarkableness as Sihar and Shenya! And, like them, may you have the chance to balance the hurtful old with the healing new, and offer a new world, even to the gods.

Until next time!

★ ★ ★

END OF BOOK II

Note

1   One cycle = 13 years.

EPILOGUE/INTRODUCTION

The Return

Boston Sky

Wanda eyes the graying clouds warily. *It's gonna pour!* She runs from the subway stop to the square brick building where she's taking "Theories of International Relations." It's their second meeting but the first, real class. The first one was all about introductions: the course, the professor, the students. It's a small group with only six students but, for a graduate seminar, it's big enough. The professor is a world-renowned scholar, although a bit past his prime. The students are a mixed lot: there's Gary, the eager white guy who spent two years in Africa with the Peace Corps; Melissa, the cynical white feminist who's into labor unions and the world's oppressed; Arjun, the skinny guy from India with the Oxbridge accent; Felicia, the equally skinny girl from Singapore, also with an Oxbridge accent (*the Commonwealth lives!*); and, perhaps most unexpectedly, Robert, an older white guy who's an instructor at West Point.

"How come you're getting a PhD in IR?" Wanda asked Robert after class.

"Well," he replied thoughtfully, "IR is about War. For those of us who have to fight wars, we are the most vested in stopping them. So I thought I'd better learn how."

"Oh!" was all she could say. How could one argue with a warrior? *Still*, Wanda wondered, *is IR only about War?*

Wanda, the Student

And then, of course, there's her. An African-American woman in her late twenties from the Midwest. She's not what white folks would consider the typical Black Woman, even after having Michelle O in the White House. Wanda's parents are well-to-do: her father's a surgeon; her mother, a homemaker. And she has two brothers, each of whom, like her, is pursuing further studies. (The older one aims to be a doctor; the younger, a communications whiz.) So they represent a kind of black bourgeois royalty. Certainly, Wanda's often accused her brothers of behaving like princes! But she takes her privilege seriously. It comes not easily. Like most black folks, a veritable United Nations runs through her veins – European, Afro-Caribbean, Native American, maybe even a dollop of Asian. Who knows for sure? This lineage did not come about because people "fell in love" and decided to "cross boundaries" by "getting married." And it's only by the sweat of his brow and the determination of his spirit that Wanda's grandfather, the son of a sharecropper, lifted himself and his family to the status of a country lawyer, able to send his son to medical school.

Still, Wanda's in IR mainly because of Auntie Ann (Americanized for Anh). She was the best thing to happen to Uncle Jake during the Vietnam War, even though he lost a leg to it. She was his doctor at the American Hospital. Once in the US, however, Auntie Ann could not get a medical license. She settled for nursing, instead. And, unable to have children of her own (a virus from the war, she vaguely explained), Auntie Ann plied Wanda and her brothers with mouth-watering delectables like chicken rice soup with lemongrass or grilled pork meatballs with sweet-and-sour peanut sauce, usually on weekends to give Wanda's parents a break. After the feasting was done and the dishes stacked in the dishwasher, Uncle Jake would turn to the newspaper and her brothers to the basketball hoop in the backyard. Wanda and Auntie Ann would sit at the kitchen table, peeling oranges and drinking tea, and just chat. Beside the food, this was Wanda's favorite part of every visit.

Auntie Ann would tell the curious and affectionate Wanda about French colonialism in Indochina – and it reminded the young girl of the transatlantic slave trade that brought her ancestors to America; about how local people had to work for the white man in the heat and dust of rubber plantations in Southeast Asia – and Wanda saw black slaves toiling in the backbreaking cotton and tobacco fields of the American South; about how learning the white man's languages, customs, and religions wiped out the peoples' own – and Wanda appreciated anew what hurdles black folks had to overcome to retain any sense of who they were. "We have much in common," Auntie Ann would sigh to Wanda.

In college, Wanda discovered other worlds of marvel and wonder. These spoke to the Native American side of her. In a course called "Indigenous Cultures of America, North and South," Wanda learned about the grand cosmovision of the peoples of the Andes, how they saw everything around them, including the mountains and the rivers and the trees, as alive and interactive and full of wisdom. Even today, advocates for social justice would rally native peoples against extractive mining companies – and the greedy officials who contracted them – by recalling the awesome power of *pachamama* or Mother Earth. It has the ability to retaliate against any violence done unto it! And the mountains would spew forth with fire and molten lava, as if on cue, taking down the mining companies and more than one comprador government along the way.

Closer to home, Wanda learned of the matriarchal societies of the First Nations where women wielded as much power as men, sometimes more, given their roles as mothers and healers. Only daughters could inherit property, and a son-in-law lived in the *tipi* with his mother-in-law until she passed away. Tribal elders also told magical stories over campfires, from one generation to the next, of animals that thought, spoke, and acted just like people, sometimes turning into people, and, more often than not, teaching people what they needed to know about surviving in the world. Different tribes each had their own traditions but they shared certain myths and icons. One was the Coyote, a trickster full of mischief as well as important lessons . . . That these traditions persisted despite the genocide, whether intended (through guns) or not (through germs), still amazes Wanda. And, like Asians and Africans, so too did Native Americans endure the whip of colonial masters who wanted them for their gold, their bodies, and their souls.

A sense of commonality and solidarity deepened in Wanda. It cut across time and space, culture and language. Blood seemed beside the point. A committed Marxist, Wanda saw capitalism as the all-determining evil.

"It's a global thing," she tells Auntie Ann, while helping herself to another deep-fried, sweet potato patty.

Instead of depression or anger, knowledge of these worlds fuels within Wanda an insatiable curiosity and sense of adventure. Not only does she rejoice in the bounty of foods and music and art and dance that these worlds convey, but Wanda also recognizes their significance. She remembers well relatives talking about how black folks, during the time of slavery, would sing and dance and beat their drums – *pom-pom-pom!* – as a way of recalling their free ancestors. This way, the slaves could experience a bit of release, if only for a while. Native peoples of what the *conquistadores* called the New World would also celebrate with drums and dancing and singing. A whole village would sway in rhythm to enjoy a night under the sparkling stars after a hard day of hunting or fishing, gathering and skinning and cooking. They recognized they were members of a larger whole whose individual parts meant something only when each works in tandem with the others. Then there's all the eating! Native cultures could stay alive, Wanda firmly believes, despite all the killing and the dying, by cooking maize in a particular way or pounding flour-bread just so. Thus, the belabored masses of Asia, Africa, and the Americas could keep an island of Self in a sea populated by Others who assume they are the only Self around.

Wanda couldn't reveal any of this when introducing herself to the class. It was too personal. She also didn't want to be branded. She'd had enough of that in college. White professors and students would turn to her, the lone minority in the class, whenever issues of "race" came up. So, on that first day, Wanda said the least to get by:

"I'm interested in comparative studies."

The Class

Thankfully, Wanda makes it into the classroom just minutes before Professor Miller does. A man in his early sixties and author of several books and articles on War and Peace, Treaties and International Organizations, the Middle East, and, of course, the Cuban Missile Crisis, Jonathan Miller looks like the prototypical Ivy League academic: bow tie, tweed jacket, flannel pants. A pipe used to complete the picture until indoor smoking was prohibited. Now Miller "smokes" his chalk. Whenever ruminating, he unconsciously puts any chalk at hand to his lips and draws on it deeply, as if. Old habits die hard.

"Some people say," Professor Miller opens the class with an attempt at humor, "that sex and politics have much in common. What do you think it is?"

Melissa, the union feminist, mutters under her breath: "Someone's always gettin' screwed!"

Sitting next to her, Wanda catches the crack and is barely able to choke down her guffaw. Miller may or may not have detected the insubordination. He's taught too many generations of graduate students to care. *They're always a little frisky in the beginning*, he dismisses.

"The answer is: somebody's always on top!"

A few giggle nervously, others audibly groan, and still others remain diplomatically silent.

Miller sallies forth. "The point is, ladies and gentlemen, International Relations is about power. And, like sex, power means A making B do what B would otherwise not do." Miller relishes the analogy. *That'll keep 'em awake!* But Wanda, like the rest of her class, can't help but wonder: *Geez, what kind of sex is this guy having?*

Miller continues oblivious and unperturbed.

Thomas Hobbes

"We begin with the Founding Fathers of IR: Thucydides, Machiavelli, and Hobbes." Students dutifully open their notebooks to take down the *guru*'s words. "I presume you've all done the readings?" Everyone nods. Satisfied, Miller continues: "Thucydides taught us about the need for balance of power when one state rises in ambition and capability compared to the others. He coined the immortal words of the Athenian generals to the people of Melos, an island that wanted to stay neutral in the war between Athens and Sparta: 'the strong do what they *can*, the weak suffer what they *must*'. Because the Melians insisted on neutrality, the Athenian generals killed all the men and enslaved the women and children. Otherwise, the generals feared, they would look weak. And if that happened, then they would have lost the war before fighting it!" Robert, the West Pointer, nods vigorously to this point. "And Machiavelli, as we all know, instructed us on the ways of the Prince. To have power – and keep it – he must be a Fox and a Lion both. The former helps him avoid snares that enemies may set for him; the latter helps him captivate his subjects with courage and charisma. Too often," Miller peers at the class piercingly, "aspiring politicians remember the Fox only and forget the Lion – to their detriment." He pauses dramatically. "But it was Hobbes –" Miller writes down (1588–1679) on the blackboard "– who gave us IR as a field of *study*, not just *practice*. He explained why men would *rationally* abandon their *absolute freedom* in the State of Nature for the *relative freedom* of Society, with its laws and punishments, as authorized by the State or what he called the Leviathan.

"According to Hobbes, a State of Nature existed prior to Society and, therefore, the State. This State of Nature was lawless, anarchical, and highly competitive. Individuals had to wage a constant 'warre of every man against every man', rendering life, in his famous description, as 'solitary, poore, nasty, brutish, and short'. Man needed to hoard all the resources he could acquire, by hook or by crook, in order to survive. But man could not continue like this indefinitely, for 'the weakest has strength enough to kill the strongest'. Why do you suppose this was so?" Miller asks the class rhetorically.

"We all have to sleep, Sir?" Gary, the Peace Corps guy, answers promptly.

"Harvey Mansfield at Harvard, I believe, has written the classic text on this," Arjun adds helpfully in his clipped English with a hint of old Calcutta.

"That's right." Miller looks at his roster of names. "Gary and Arjun, is it?" Both nod keenly in response. *It's nice when they're still fresh and impressionable*, Miller observes. *Saves a lot of time later on.* The professor continues: "Yes, even the strongest man has to sleep, thereby leaving him vulnerable to attack by even the weakest man. But before we go on, please call me Jonathan. We go by a first-name basis here to give a semblance of democracy." He chuckles at the wryness of it all but the class seems immune to humor this morning. *First-semester-first-years*, he rationalizes, *there's only so much one can do.* Miller moves on.

"But Hobbes regarded Man as inherently endowed with Reason. It was this faculty that enabled Man to form a *social contract* with other individuals, thereby inaugurating the State/Leviathan. Its main purpose: to adjudicate disputes so individuals would not have to bop one another over the head in their sleep – Yes?" Melissa, the union feminist, has raised her hand.

"How is the social contract rational when Hobbes excludes women and children? He counts them with 'chattall' as the kind of possessions men bring with them from the State of Nature to Society. Isn't his whole conjecture sexist?"

Miller puffs on his chalk.

"Yes, feminists have critiqued Hobbes for assuming individuals to be men only. He famously analogized individuals to mushrooms sprouting after a rain. In other words, they have no families, no languages, no society of any kind. But let's keep to the original text, shall we, Melinda?"

"Melissa."

"Uh, yes. I believe there's a course on Hobbes in Women's Studies. You could discuss that matter more fully there. Now where were we? Ah, yes. Escape from the State of Nature to form Society under the authority of the Leviathan."

Melissa refrains from asking any more questions. She also stops taking notes.

"So you see," Miller blithely goes on, "how contemporary IR maps onto Hobbes: the international arena is like the State of Nature since there is no global Leviathan to ensure an International Society of law among individuals, now seen as States."

"What about international norms like the Geneva Convention?" Robert the West Pointer asks. "Don't they mitigate the international arena as a State of Nature?"

Miller's eyes light up. These are the kind of questions he likes.

"Of course, there are some who argue – we call them the English School – that the world may be approaching the kind of social contract Hobbes envisioned for the Leviathan. Trouble is, these conventions have no binding authority since there is no global Leviathan to enforce them."

Robert nods vigorously again but Gary looks down at his notes with knitted brows.

"Isn't a global Leviathan what many would call a global hegemon? Isn't that the US today?" Felicia the Singaporean asks trenchantly.

"Yes, well, let's reserve discussions of US foreign policy for another day, shall we?" Miller dodges expertly. "Let us first establish our foundational concepts before jumping on to critiques."

Felicia writes coolly but stiffly in her notes.

Miller continues: "Now back to Hobbes. His *real* contribution, I would suggest, lies in his analytical *method*. After all, IR can take any shape or form, depending on time and circumstance. For example, the world used to be dominated by monarchies. Today, secular governments comprise the majority of States. With his method, Hobbes develops a *science* of the international. Note how he begins *The Leviathan* with naming." Miller puts on his glasses and reads. "'*So that in the right Definition of Names, lyes the first use of Speech; which is the Acquisition of Science.*' That is, Hobbes sets up a framework for knowing before he identifies what is to be known. Um, yes?" Miller notices the young woman at the far end of the seminar table has raised her hand.

Another Kind of Question

"Excuse me, Sir, but this was the part that confused me the most," Wanda begins. "For example, in *The Leviathan*, he writes the following about dreams:

> *. . . And because waking I often observe the absurdity of Dreames, but never dream of the absurdities of my waking Thoughts; I am well satisfied, that being awake, I know I dreame not; though when I dreame, I think my selfe awake.*

"And?"

"This suggests that dreams have no connection with real life."

"And?"

"Well, uh, there are other traditions, besides Freudian," Wanda hastens to add, "that treat dreams differently. They are seen as a source of wisdom or a way to decipher signs . . ."

"Of course," Miller retorts, "plenty of superstitions have such notions . . ."

"But excuse me, Sir," Wanda finds her words tumbling out a little faster than usual, "it's not just superstition. For example, this woman of Wampanoag descent had the same dream three nights in a row. She couldn't understand it at first because the characters in her dream seemed to be speaking a foreign language. But they were the ancestors she recognized from old family photos. Then she realized they were speaking to her in Wôpanâak, her people's language now almost extinct. So she started a language reclamation project. Later, she received a MacArthur genius award for it and the project is now housed across the street at MIT." Wanda pauses, a little breathless. *What am I doing?* But she can't stop. She has to say what she is saying – and more.

"That's all very nice but let's return to the main text –" Miller seeks to deflect this sudden torrent of words and thoughts and feelings, so unusual for a first-semester-first-year.

"I'm sorry, Sir," Wanda barrels on, as if caught in a landslide. "But I also had real problems with how Hobbes identifies the State of Nature. In particular, he refers to the 'savages' of America as an example." She reads from her copy of *Leviathan*, heavily underlined in red. "He writes:

> *For the savage people in many places of America, except the government of small Families, the concord whereof dependeth on naturall lust, have no government at all; and live at this day in that brutish manner, as I said before.*

"And, again, he states in *De Cive* –" she turns to a small, thin volume, equally smattered in red ink "– here:

> *They of America are Examples hereof, even in this present Age: Other Nations have been in former Ages, which now indeed are become Civill, and Flourishing, but were then few, fierce, short-lived, poor, nasty, and destroy'd of all that Pleasure, and Beauty of life, which Peace and Society are wont to bring with them.*

"But this doesn't at all describe what native societies were like!"

Pushmataha's Speech

Echoing in Wanda's mind are the words of the great Choctaw leader Pushmataha. He argued against going to war with the American settlers, as urged by the Shawnee Tecumseh, to unite the eastern tribes against the encroaching whites. Wanda always felt that one could debate whether Pushmataha's strategy was ultimately successful or not, but one cannot deny the eloquence of his ethics about honor and friendship and not breaking treaties – especially given the lack of such from the US government:

> *My friends and fellow countrymen! You now have no just cause to declare war against the American people, or wreak your vengeance upon them as enemies, since they have ever manifested feelings of friendship towards you. It is besides inconsistent with your national glory and with your honor, as a people, to violate your solemn treaty; and a disgrace to the memory of your forefathers, to wage war against the American people merely to gratify the malice of the English . . .*
>
> *Be not, I pray you, guilty of rashness, which I never as yet have known you to be; therefore, I implore you, while healing measures are in the election of us all, not to break the treaty, nor violate your pledge or honor, but to submit our grievances, whatever they may be, to the Congress of the United States, according to the articles of the treaty existing between us and the American people . . .*
>
> *From tempers equally balanced let it be known we are warm in the field of battle, and cool in the hours of debate . . .*

Miller's Response

Miller surveys his class. The other students are all looking at him with questioning, doubtful eyes. He imagines what must be going through their heads: *Maybe the old geezer doesn't have it anymore. Why should we listen to him? Let's drop this class! Death to the Old Order! Long live the New Order!* He cannot have such chaos so early in the term. He must take back control.

"Thank you for your insights, uh, Wanda, is it?" Miller interjects icily. "But this is a class on *International Relations*, not Native American culture." With that, he lectures for the remaining two hours, broaching no insurrection other than questions for information or clarification only.

Wanda leaves the class devastated. Each student rushes off to the next class or activity but Wanda wonders if her cohorts are avoiding her. *Why won't anyone speak to me? Why was the professor so hard on me?* Miller's classroom, it seems, is more State of Nature than the wilds of America. *Why can't I keep my big mouth shut?! Now I'll never get into the PhD program!*

Racing through Wanda's mind now are the stipulations of the program, made so very plain at orientation: one-third of the entering class is not invited back after the first year. A doctoral student is expensive to support! Those who make it can go on for two more years of course work, then they must take an exam to see if they qualify to write a dissertation, then it's the dissertation itself. Once that's done, usually taking up a year or three, they'd have to defend their work with a panel of judges made up of tough, crusty faculty like Jonathan Miller. *I'm doomed!* Wanda sees all her aspirations for a life of meaning and action, learning and teaching fading away agonizingly, bit by bit . . .

Wind and rain pelt the campus. Thunder booms loudly and too closely for comfort. But Wanda trudges on in a daze. What rages inside her far exceeds the elements battling on the outside.

The Library

Not realizing how or why, Wanda finds herself, soaked from head to toe, standing in front of a library. It's the smallest one on campus but with big windows glowing warmth and learning from the inside. Wanda cannot resist and enters. She flops into one of the friendly, overstuffed armchairs by the door, dripping a pool of misery onto the colorful area rug.

An ancient librarian with a laughing face comes by, rolling a trolley of books. *He's probably going to ask me to leave*, Wanda suspects defensively. *I'm making too much of a mess here.* Instead, Wanda hears a friendly voice call out:

"Lo, there! You could use a towel." And he hands her a freshly laundered, fluffy towel from his trolley.

Where did he . . . ? Wanda can't believe it. But neither does she refuse the towel. It helps to dry off, especially her sopping-wet jeans.

"Come," the ancient librarian motions to her. "My office is just around the corner. You look like you could use a cup of tea."

Normally, Wanda does not take to strangers well. Even life in Cleveland requires street smarts! But this ancient librarian seems harmless. She follows him to his glass-encased office located just behind the checkout desk. *Nothing can happen here*, Wanda ascertains.

Her eye instantly picks up a couple of unusual items. What looks like a walking stick leans against one of the bookshelves. Twisted and long, it appears, nonetheless, quite durable. On a shelf near the walking stick is a large, round bowl, slightly chipped along the edge. *He must collect antiques*, Wanda guesses.

Meanwhile, the ancient librarian busies with the tea. Eventually, he hands over a mug of steaming revival to a grateful Wanda.

"You seemed upset just now," he probes lightly, while reaching for a tin of biscuits and opens it. "Is it just the weather?" He offers her the box.

Never one to turn down a cookie, Wanda takes one and bites it gingerly.

"I wish . . ." *How do I say all that I want to say? What I feel?*

"Boyfriend troubles?" the ancient librarian tests merrily.

"I wish!" Wanda rolls her eyes. She takes a sip of tea and musters a half-truth: "I had a bit of a tussle with my professor this morning."

"Ah!" the ancient librarian chuckles. "Intellectual troubles."

"Yes!" Wanda springs to life. "How'd you guess?"

"My dear," the ancient librarian responds, "I'm a university librarian. That's like being a bartender at the neighborhood pub."

For the first time all day, Wanda allows herself a laugh.

"Tell me," the ancient librarian prompts, "what happened?"

And Wanda finds herself unloading the morning's exchange: what Miller said, what she said, how she couldn't help saying what she said, how Miller shut her down, how nobody spoke to her afterwards, how she felt like an alien from outer space. Wanda ends her long, sorry tale with a deep sigh.

"Now I've ruined any chance of ever getting into the PhD program." Wanda looks into her empty mug, wishing more than tea could fill it.

"Don't be so hard on yourself," the ancient librarian assures her cheerfully. "And don't be so hard on the professor. His job is to stimulate debate. He wants to see who can measure up, who can't. Give him some credit and give yourself some, too."

Wanda looks at the librarian searchingly. The same torrent of words and thoughts and feelings that seized her earlier in the morning threatens to seize her again.

"But do I want to be in this program that teaches all this stuff that I disagree with so much? IR doesn't have to be about war and competition and anarchy *only* – men fighting other men all the time while shunting women and children off to huddle with the cattle. People are not like mushrooms after a rain! The State of Nature for indigenous peoples – *my* people – has always been powerful yet loving, challenging but nurturing. How could people survive *without* what Mother Earth has given us – and still gives us – despite all our transgressions and arrogance?" Wanda looks down and lowers her voice. "More than that, I wonder if I have what it takes to make it as a grad student. I don't want to be assaulted at every turn, if this morning is any indication of what's ahead. It's a kind of violence that professors mistake for 'intellectual rigor'. Intellectual *rigor mortis* is more like it!

"In college, I thought we could better people's lives by emancipating them from the shackles of capitalism. Now I realize we need to emancipate them from the shackles of their ideas! It's not just what we do but also how we *think*. If we believe the State of Nature is 'solitary, poore, nasty, brutish, and short', then no amount of protesting and demonstrating, reforming and legislating could bring about real change. People will remain locked in their minds by their minds. And who benefits from *that*? Obviously, the powerful and the mighty." A half-snort erupts from Wanda. "Then, again, who am I to challenge the status quo? To have all these big ideas and big ambitions? I mean, *how do I know what I know – and what I want to know – is worth knowing?*"

A Dog-eared Paperback

The ancient librarian listens patiently until all has spilled forth from Wanda and she has nothing more to unburden. He fishes a book from the piles on his desk. It's a dog-eared paperback, clearly long abused by undergraduates.

"Here." The ancient librarian tosses the book to Wanda. "This might help." With that, he returns to his trolley of books. "Must get back to work!" He waves a happy good-bye and rolls on to destinations unknown.

Surprised by his abrupt departure, Wanda continues to sit in the librarian's office, looking out the window at the furious wind and rain. *I could make a run for it.* Then she realizes she's still holding the book he gave her. She has no intention of reading yet another volume, especially one not assigned on her syllabus.

But sheer curiosity moves her to flip it open, past the Preface and the Foreword, to the main text. The opening line seems to speak directly to her: "Hello, Gentle Friend! . . ." And Wanda finds herself increasingly drawn into the story. As she does so, she hears the distant *pom-pom-pom* of her ancestors' drums, pounding in pace with the beating of her heart . . .

> . . . *we are warm in the field of battle, and cool in the hours of debate* . . .

BEGINNING OF *SIHAR & SHENYA*

QUESTIONS FOR DISCUSSION

Book I: The Orchid and the Tree

1. What's the meaning of "the orchid and the tree"? What is the role that nature plays in the fable?
2. How does each character change in the story? From what to what? What enables the change?
3. What's the mantra on *karma*? How does it play out for the characters?
4. What's the implication of transformation for IR theory? Realists claim that transformation is not possible, only changes in who's on top, who's on the bottom: the fundamental system of power relations remains the same. What do you think of this proposition after reading this story?

Book II: The Laughing Monk's Bet

1. What's the notion of Time in this story?
2. What does it mean that the Laughing Monk can travel between the Human World and the Mystical World? That there is a Mystical World in the first place? That the Mythic Ones "play" with human lives that, in effect, represent them?

3. Who in Book I is reincarnated from whom in Book II? What do these reincarnations suggest?

4. What is the debt owed by which characters to whom? How is this debt repaid twenty lifetimes later? What are the implications of this way of thinking, doing, being, and relating for IR theory and practice?

Epilogue/Introduction: The Return

1. What are the differences between Wanda's exposure to international relations and Miller's teaching of it? Does the difference matter? If so, to whom and why?

2. Is Wanda simply being unrealistic in her pursuit of a graduate degree in IR? Maybe she should study Anthropology or Sociology, instead?

3. Is Miller a bad professor? How else could Miller have responded to Felicia, Melissa, and Wanda? How might this have affected student engagement?

4. What's the significance of Wanda hearing the beating of her ancestors' drums – *pom-pom-pom* – at the end of the Epilogue/Introduction?

5. What does "the return" mean here? What are its implications for IR theory?

Overall

1. What's the role of the Laughing Monk? Is there a Laughing Monk counterpart in IR, as theory and practice?

2. Who are the Mythic Ones, if any at all, in Book I and the Epilogue/Introduction?

3. What if you read the whole work out of order? What new insights would arise, if any?

4. What new perspectives have you gained from this work as a whole? Could you apply these perspectives to your own life? To IR?

5. What do you think the author's objective was in writing this work and in this way?